Black & Tan

BLACK & TAN

*A Collection of Essays and Excursions
on Slavery, Culture War, and Scripture in America*

Douglas Wilson

canonpress
Moscow, Idaho

Published by Canon Press
P.O. Box 8729, Moscow, ID 83843
800-488-2034 | www.canonpress.com

Douglas Wilson, *Black and Tan: A Collection of Essays and Excursions on Slavery, Culture War, and Scripture in America*
Copyright © 2005 by Douglas Wilson

Printed in the United States of America.
Cover design by Paige Atwood.
Scripture quotations are taken from the Authorized (King James) Version.

Library of Congress Cataloging-in-Publication Data

Wilson, Douglas, 1953-
    Black and tan : a collection of essays and excursions on slavery, culture war, and scripture in America / by Douglas Wilson.
        p. cm.
    ISBN-13: 978-1-59128-032-3 (alk. paper)
    ISBN-10: 1-59128-032-X (alk. paper)
    1. Slavery and the church--Southern States--History. 2. Slavery--Moral and ethical aspects--Southern States--History. 3. Slavery--Southern States--History. 4. Southern States--History--1775-1865. 5. Southern States--Race relations. 6. Southern States--Religious life and customs. 7. Christianity and culture--Southern States--History. 8. Culture conflict--Southern States--History. 9. United States--History--Civil War, 1861-1865--Social aspects. I. Title.

    E441.W75 2005
    306.3'62'0973--dc22

                            2005012542

09 10 11 12 13 14 15   9 8 7 6 5 4 3 2

Contents

Foreword
by Nathan Wilson

I DRANK MY FIRST black and tan in Annapolis, Maryland, my father's hometown. It was poured in the American style, Bass Ale on the bottom and then Guinness, poured carefully over a bent spoon to avoid breaking the layer and mixing the two beers. Across the Atlantic, those tending bar generally chuck the spoon and let the beers blend. The taste is more interesting, but the look less artistic. Regardless of technique, the combination is a lovely one.

In America, our particular blend of races came about through great hypocrisy, in both the North and South. The slave trade was nothing but wickedness. To be a little simplistic: the South wanted to end the trade, but not the slavery, and the North wanted to blame the South for providing the market for the kidnapped souls the North was importing. The whole history and categorization of our various racial hypocrisies is not something I am capable of exploring here. God judged both North and South with the bloodiest of our wars. God judged this nation, and it is impossible to deny that He has continued to do so as we reap various fruits of sinful segregation and of the equally sinful attempts at expiating our guilt through statist salvation. There is much to lament on the subject of race relations, but I find that God has not only judged us. He has blessed us as well; He has blessed all our races, for example, with a great mixed beer.

I am quite grateful for my own ethnic ancestors, in all their Celticness, but I am also grateful that some of their contributions are where they are: behind me, across the ocean, safely tucked away in graves. They have contributed an attitude to America, a fighting spirit and an individualism that have been both a blessing and a curse. But there is nothing in the idea of a "pure" Celtic America that I love. Bass Ale is fine enough, but I have no desire to go back to drinking it isolated safely in its own glass.

Growing up my father's son, I was taught the love of many things. I can think fondly of ancestral plaid and bagpipes, but my affection for blues and jazz runs just as deep or deeper. I am extremely grateful to have grown up in a culture influenced and altered by the juxtaposition of races, and even more so because I believe my children and grandchildren will grow up in a culture where that juxtaposition has been more fruitful, and the mutual influences increased.

I love peanut butter. And lest anyone accuse me of being trite or superficial in my praise, it is hardly superficial to me. I would guess that roughly seventy-five percent of the cells that my body has produced over the course of my life have been made out of George Washington Carver's magical invention. I think that percentage is higher for my father. I love the music that came out of the South and the effect it has had on our national personality. I love athletics and the unique personality they have gained by the mixture of races; segregated basketball was about as interesting as a PTA meeting. Jesse Owens showed up Hitler's lie, single-handedly, when nations, theologians, and philosophers failed—and he wore our flag. Some would want deeper cultural acknowledgments from me than this, again accusing me of being superficial, but the trouble is that such things only appear to be superficial. I have been shaped by these things, as we all have. Our culture has been impacted in deep and profound ways by such juxtapositions and will continue to be. So the curse connected to slavery, the sin of our white fathers against our black fathers, has come back to bless us. It has shaped every aspect of what it means to be American, and is part of why being an

American is still worthwhile. The blessings have always been there, for the culture, for the Church, and some of the greatest of white sins have come in the arrogance of trying to reject those blessings.

But this is not simply a blind or romantic view of race. There has been a great deal of hypocrisy and faithlessness in our racial history—and the traffic has gone both ways. Hatred and bitterness has played a major role for many on both sides. But beyond that, in humility and faithfulness, comes the blessing of the God of paradox, the God who raises the dead. A once white country is no longer white, having been broadened and strengthened by the victims of its white fathers. And as for those first slaves: their descendants, while still sometimes held down by their own sins and residual paganism, not to mention the sins of others against them, have been blessed by being part of this culture. This is why a secular approach to racial reconciliation will always be doomed. Throughout our history, God has brought many blessings to the blacks as well, at the center of which was access to the gospel. The tragedy of pagan Africa was more significant than the tragedy of Southern slavery.

In Christ, whites are a blessing to blacks. In Christ, blacks are a blessing to whites. In our history, there has been more than a little of this. But apart from Christ, our races are simply a snare and temptation to one another. So I look forward to the final America, to the final Church, the Church that spans cultures, nations, and ethnic boundaries. I look forward to descendants as affected by a Christian Africa as by a once-upon-a-time Christian Europe. When it comes to culture, pour me a black and tan into the glass of the Christian faith.

No need to use a spoon.

Introduction

I AM THE PASTOR of a Reformed church in the Pacific Northwest, where I have served since 1977. As this ministry has developed over the years, I have to confess that history keeps getting tangled up in it. I have written two historical biographies[1] for the general reader, and a number of years ago we began hosting an annual history conference that now draws about nine hundred people.

This sort of coloring outside the lines has excited comment in some quarters, and in response to some of my critics, I have sometimes sought to minimize my historical credentials. In this I have simply and cheerfully acknowledged that I am not trained as a professional historian. I do not have a graduate degree in history, and as a general rule I do not make my living through dealing with historical topics. I have claimed that I am a popularizer and a storyteller. I was once speaking with Dr. Harold O. J. Brown about the late Francis Schaeffer, and he used the *appreciative* image of a caricaturist. I have used that same description for myself, not wanting to be seen as claiming more for myself than I ought to. I did this because I don't mind when people see me as more of "a preacher" than a historian. I *am* a preacher.

1. *For Kirk and Covenant: The Stalwart Courage of John Knox* (Nashville: Highland Books, 2000), and *Beyond Stateliest Marble: The Passionate Femininity of Anne Bradstreet* (Nashville: Highland Books, 2001).

But all preachers must also be historians in some sense, because we preach from the Bible, most of which is sacred history. The center of our faith is the resurrection of Jesus Christ, an event in *history*. When a professional historian sidles up to me and says that the event did not happen, it doesn't even slow me down. When a professional theologian tells me that what actually matters is the Christ-event in the preaching of the *kerygma*, and not whether He actually rose, I cheerfully retreat into my best imitation of a fundamentalist. When a professional postmodernist says that Christian doctrine functions as the "grammar" of our Christian system, just as English grammar functions for English speakers, without any reference to meta-truth, I draw the necessary conclusion that all these professionals are overpaid. The resurrection of Christ defines history, and not the other way around. The central Christian confession—the Apostles' Creed—is full of historical claims, and ministers are the appointed guardians of those claims. At any moment, a trained historian might come into the Garden and say, "Yea, hath God said?"

This ministerial responsibility is not limited to sacred history. I would want to argue further that ministers have a responsibility to be amateur historians of the *post*-apostolic era because they need to know what Wesleyans are, why we Protestants don't believe that Rome is the one true church, why people "go forward" at revival meetings, why America thinks it is all right to conduct murder by the million as long as the victims are unborn, and why some Christians think it is a sin to drink beer. All of this involves the study of uninspired history, and all of it is directly related to a minister's job description. So, while I am always happy to learn how to perform this task better than I do, I do not see that it is possible for me to abandon it without abandoning my ministerial post.

Therefore I see one of my tasks as that of being a ministerial popularizer of history. But no one, not even a popularizer, has the right to get his facts wrong and maintain that Columbus sailed the ocean blue in 1498. It is not accurate, and it doesn't rhyme. A popularizer is one who makes difficult material intelligible to a wide audience; he is not one who is ill-informed himself, making things up as he goes along. The name for *that* is demagogue, not popularizer. But sometimes a popularizer can be assumed to be just winging it—perhaps because the people can understand him, or perhaps because he gave a history conference and somebody came. In my case, such an assumption would be erroneous. Please bear with me, because I genuinely dislike having to talk like this. "I say again, Let no man think me a fool; if otherwise, yet as a fool receive me, that I may boast myself a little" (2 Cor. 11:16). Since 1979, I have maintained a consistent pattern of reading a heap of books covering a wide range of subjects, including history, theology, biography, commentary, literature, social criticism, philosophy, poetry, and so on, for which I received not an iota of institutional credit. This makes me an uncertified *generalist*—not to mention a loose cannon on deck—and my previous comments should simply be taken as disavowing any particular training as a historical *specialist*. But even so, as a generalist, I need to say (if it's "myself what says it") that I am a reasonably well-informed one. I do not read narrowly, simply reading "party-line" materials which agree with my preconceived notions. What I learn from this kind of reading is what I undertake to "popularize." I am not making up stuff as I go.

At the same time, the fact that I am willing to teach on historical subjects does not mean that I somehow think I am infallible. I have been wrong on numerous points over the years—sometimes the mistake is mine, and sometimes a source leads me astray. The point of all this is simply to say that on such subjects I am always open to correction, and moreover I am eager for it. But given the nature of the case, that correction is not likely to come from refereed journals. Rather, it will occur when someone saunters up to me after a talk and says that he never knew that Tamerlane was a Swede.

So what does the ministerial task have to do with *American* history? More details on this will come in the pages to follow, but perhaps the relevance can be illustrated by taking a look at the future. Suppose Christians two hundred years from now are being embarrassed with stories about the old evil days when their

twisted twentieth-century Christian ancestors blew up abortion
clinics, shot abortion doctors, mailed anthrax to abortion clinics,
etc. "That's all they ever did, day in and day out," the instruc-
tor said calmly, finishing his lecture. Now the Bible condemns all
these murderous activities, and it is not necessary for our future
brother to reject this slander of us and our peaceful pro-life activities in order for him to stand for the *abstract* truth that the Bible
condemns murder. But in fact, it remains a slander of twentieth-
century pro-life Christians, and *if* he accepts it, it is highly likely
that he has been completely outmaneuvered by his enemies for
strategic reasons, reasons that are pertinent to *their* controversies.
He sadly concludes that a hypothetical opposition to abortion is
possible in some utopian situation, but alas, not in this world. We
believe ourselves to be currently in an analogous situation.

If we want to understand the culture wars of the twentieth and
twenty-first centuries, we must come to grips with the culture wars
of the nineteenth century. In order to do this, it is necessary to
get clear on the nature of American slavery, which was *not* what its
abolitionist opponents claimed for it. If it had been, it is hard to
see how the biblical instructions could have been applicable—for
example, I would not cite I Timothy 6:1–4 to a person trying to
escape from a Nazi death camp. "Obey the existing authorities!"
But if antebellum slavery was the normal kind of sinful situation
that Christians have had to deal with regularly down through history (e.g., one comparable to what Paul, Philemon, and Onesimus
had to address), then the instructions in I Timothy 6 make perfect
sense. We need to learn that the antebellum situation was one of
Normal Sin, not one of Apocalyptic Evil.

That our nation did not remove slavery in the *way* it ought to
have been removed helps to explain many of our nation's problems in dealing with contemporary social evils. Those evils include
abortion-on-demand, radical feminism, and rampant sodomy. In
the pursuit of our constitutional rights, we have legally executed
over forty million unborn children in this nation, and we are about
to be oppressed with sodomite marriage. We have done this under

the "protections" of the Constitution. *When in our history did we take the wrong turn that allowed the Constitution to be abused in this grotesque fashion?* Christians need to learn to argue that the events resulting in the cataclysm of 1861–1865 had something to do with it, which I believe is incontrovertible.

In dealing with these issues, it is not possible to "get at" the worldview aspects of all this in the same way you can get at the 2004 platform of the Republican Party. A lot of reading and meditating is involved, and to grasp the central issues, it is necessary to be steeped in a particular intellectual tradition. The Southern conservative intellectual tradition does not put out a periodic newsletter with bulleted talking points, but there is an identifiable position there nonetheless. When critics are as unsympathetic *to this frame of mind* as many of them have been, I honestly do not believe that detailed explanations will get through to them.

This lack of sympathy is revealed by snatching at words and highlighting inflammatory quotations. For example, in response to one critic, I agreed with him that meticulous analysis was necessary for good history but that it was not sufficient. In my letter I said this:

> Now when war comes upon a nation, the people involved in the political turmoil have to make a decision about whether they will go off and start shooting at other people, and they do not have the luxury of making that decision with all the research available to the professional historian. In some ways, such research would simply get in the way of making an honorable decision.

My questioner then claimed that I had once said that the facts alone were necessary, though not sufficient. Then he said I claimed that facts can get in the way. And this, he said, was of "monumental epistemological importance."

What was actually happening was that his paradigmatic blinders were preventing him from seeing the basic facts of what I actually said. When I agreed that meticulous analysis was necessary, I was talking about *historians*. When I said that facts can get in the way, I was talking about ordinary people who have the burden of *making* history.

The point of my letter was that if there is a young Christian today in a typical evangelical church who is thinking about joining the Marines and going to Iraq, he does not have to get a Ph.D. in American foreign policy studies first. He can make an honorable decision without that. Now this has ramifications for the study of history, but I am in no way commending it as a basic method of studying history. An infantryman doesn't need to be a historian to help make history. But historians should be competent historians as they study it, and in their study, meticulous attention to the facts matters. At the same time, "competence" cannot be defined from some neutral place. There is no detached realm of "neutral facts" where believer and unbeliever alike can go and find the pristine data. This is not a historical claim; it is a theological claim about history.

We are called to live our lives in a way that realizes there is a world outside the academy. Most of the people in the economy are not economists. Most people who have made history are not historians. Suppose the young man mentioned above came to me for pastoral counsel: "Should I join the Marines?" What would *I* need to have under my belt in order to give godly counsel? A Ph.D. in American foreign policy? Suppose someone wants to shoot abortionists so that he can be the next John Brown. As a pastor, what do I need to have read before I can say, "No, John Brown was an evil man"?

A man once asked me for pastoral counsel on whether he should talk to a nearby factory about software he had developed, software that might cost a significant number of factory workers their jobs. Do I need a graduate degree in economics? Which school? Austrian? Keynesian? How do I give honorable, biblical counsel? I know a few people who do not believe in getting immunizations. Suppose some of them get diphtheria? Do I need to go to medical school? Now, in all these areas, if I give counsel I should give *informed* counsel to the best of my ability—despite the mistakes that I will no doubt make. And the possibility of such mistakes does not require that I go to every conceivable graduate school before giving pastoral (and therefore authoritative and "dogmatic") counsel. Who is sufficient for these things?

As a generalist teaching about history, should I be open to the corrective input of specialists? Of course, and this is entirely reasonable—it would unreasonable not to be open to it. I consistently turn to specialists in various areas when my responsibilities as a pastor overlap with theirs. To take my earlier example, I *commonly* check with Christian friends who are medical doctors about any number of questions that come up in the course of my pastoral responsibilities—views on alternative medicine within the church, home-birthing, and so on. I do not begrudge this; rather, I count on it. I *often* turn to others who have greater expertise than I do in various areas, including theology, biblical languages, law, philosophy, and so on. I am a generalist, as I said at the beginning, and I have many friends with more specialized knowledge than I have. But I come to them as an informed generalist, and they receive me as such, and gladly help me out. But if I knew a Christian medical doctor who (for whatever reason) misread my words, actions, and intentions as consistently as some of my historical critics have done, it would be difficult to turn to him, even if he had expertise I could possibly use, because I would get into more tangles than I would get solutions and help. The temptation would be to wonder if I could trust his reading of medical journals if he did such a consistently poor job of reading *me*.

This brings me back to my central theme in this introduction— the propriety of ordinary people making and reading history, along with the necessity of Christian ministers leading their churches and teaching their congregations how to think about history. One evening not long ago, my wife and I had my parents to dinner, and we had a delightful time at the table with them telling stories to our boarders. Most of these were stories I have heard my entire life, and some of them I had *told* on numerous occasions. As I listened, I was delighted to hear new details, have gaps filled in, and here and there have adjustments made.

History is storytelling. Faithful history is faithful storytelling. Scripture requires parents to tell their children the story (and not to send them to grad school for it). But even here it is amazing how many little errors and emphases can go wrong in just the course of one generation. My parents told the story of how my father's life was spared when his destroyer hit a mine in the Korean War. We heard about how Corrie ten Boom joined them on the last part of their honeymoon in Japan. (And when I was a little kid, Corrie ten Boom gave me a wiffle ball, which I frankly admit I should have kept better track of, perhaps putting it in a glass case.)

As a family recollects all the assorted things that have happened, and as they pass them on to subsequent generations, it is easy to see how memories get blurry, details get hazy, and perspectives vary.

This being the case, where do we get off having a history conference every year? How can I *write* about history? If I am not exactly sure what *I* was doing in 1959, then why would I undertake to talk about events in the nineteenth century? But for a decade now, we have had an annual history conference in February. None of the speakers at this conference is a "trained historian." And this coming year, the history conference will be moved to August, rolled into a bigger event called the Trinity Festival, and we will do it all again. What are we doing? We are telling stories, and the reason we are doing so is that we believe that God requires it of us.

History depends on the dedicated historians and archivists who sort, assemble, and work through the mountains of material available to them. And when they have done their work, they present to the layman . . . mountains of material. Not only does it appear that we need specialists to deal with the raw material, we also need specialists to sort out the finished products. What is a "definitive" biography? Who says?

Scripture tells us that every fact should be confirmed in the mouth of two or three witnesses, and that in the multitude of counselors there is wisdom. Historical laymen should read broadly enough to make sure they are not reading some truncated account or other, but neither should they be embarrassed by the necessity of popularizing the material. Parents who home school have to make decisions about curricular material. Parents who serve on the curriculum committee of their children's private Christian school have to decide between this textbook and that one. They may do so in all faithfulness, despite the obvious limitations.

Those textbooks will tell the story a certain way. Andrew Jackson will either look good or he will not look good. The American colonists were either violating Romans 13 in their revolt against King George III or they were not. Cromwell was either a disaster or he wasn't. And the textbook will lean one way or the other. Everyone who undertakes this kind of task is in way over his head, and this includes the trained historians. We cannot protect ourselves by means of our own prowess.

This means that we walk by faith, faith in the God who orders all history to His own perfect ends. Trusting Him does not mean that we throw up our hands in a "facts be damned" sort of way and choose some sort of relativistic history that "works for us." Such postmodern relativism has to be rejected outright. But so does modernist hubris. No one man knows *exactly* what happened at the battle of Waterloo—although we can get the general drift of it. We are not omniscient, and so we must trust the God who is.

One other element has to be mentioned. Just as we trust Him, we also read the story with our loyalties intact. In other words, we cannot love God without loving those whom we believe to be His sons and daughters, and our brothers and sisters. I read the story of Latimer and Ridley while identifying with them. I am pulling for John Knox and not for Mary, Queen of Scots. We are a people, and so we must tell the stories of *our people* to our children. We are not given the option of being silent. And to step out in faith like this is not hubris but rather humility.

Humility is hard. In order to look back at the past, we have to (metaphorically) turn our backs on the future. This means, among other things, that the future can sneak up on us. Our study of history can mean that we give way to an optical illusion—we think we are standing on a fixed promontory, called the present, and before us extends the broad vistas supplied to us by the monthly selection of the History Book Club. But the present is never a fixed point. As C. S. Lewis pointed out in his dedication to *The Allegory of Love*, the present is also "a period": "Above all, the friend to whom I have dedicated the book, has taught me not to patronize the past, and has trained me to see the present as itself a 'period.'"[2] We are always standing on the fantail of a moving ship. Future thinkers and historians will one day be staring at us with furrowed brow, with the same baffled expression that *we* wear when looking at Sir Philip Sidney in his Elizabethan ruff.

But if the present is a historical period, then some of the things that we think are slam-dunk certainties will almost certainly turn out not to be. E. G. Stanley once commented (with some acidity) that the history of scholarship is the history of error. And was it Max Planck who said that science advances funeral by funeral? And Malcolm Muggeridge once said that evolution will be shown to have been one of the great jokes of history. Scholarship of all kinds—scientific, historical, grammatical, philosophical—partakes fully in the tendency the human race has to veer into sin and folly. Some of the dumbest ideas ever to afflict us have been embraced *first* in the academy and abandoned there *last*. Two examples should suffice—Marxism and evolution. Marxists think it can cost a dollar to make a loaf of bread, and that they can make people sell it for fifty cents, and then still have bread. There are people in our university system who *still* think that. And evolutionists think that the Canadian moose and the bright yellow canary are blood cousins. Where are you *most* likely to find people who will defend such things? The answer is some place where people have letters after their names.

But the established historical guild knows how to defend itself. Objectivity is a false god, and the worship of this idol is particularly pernicious in disciplines like journalism and history. It is not possible to be objective—although of course it *is* possible to be honest.

---

2. C. S. Lewis, *The Allegory of Love* (Oxford: Oxford Univ. Press, 1936), viii.

By pretending to attain to objectivity, a writer's fundamental faith commitments are not eliminated, but rather submerged—and they then come out in interesting and intellectually dishonest ways.

The study of history is largely a study of sinning, and usually the sinning is on a grand scale involving armies, navies, courtesans, synods, backstabbing, running for Congress, and more. There is the occasional hero, but there is also the hapless character that we might identify as hero fodder. Since everyone likes and admires heroes, sometimes they have to be manufactured for the sake of posterity.

To complicate the picture, the historians doing the study are sinners themselves. Some have embraced the sin and have gone over to the "dark side of the force," and so they tell us lie after lie about what happened before we got here. Other historians are conscientious Christians, and they seek to grow in their own personal sanctification as they take on the important task of writing our stories. It makes a difference whether Moses or Jeroboam writes the history curriculum. Some historians sin through hagiography and others sin through debunking. Some strive to be godly while hacking their way through a hagiographic jungle (with the machete of truth) and others strive for godliness as they fight the cynical postmodern debunkers.

The Christian who wants to be faithful here has to be very careful because the boundaries of the acceptable are always vigorously policed. We have all heard about political correctness, but after about a hundred years or so, it turns into historical correctness. The guild does a good job (for the most part) in dealing with the occasional crank who offers up the theory that Robert E. Lee was a space alien. But the guild also does a good job in ostracizing anyone who differs from the current reigning orthodoxy, whatever that orthodoxy may happen to be (and there always *is* one). And so it is that the lunatic and the "heretic" often find themselves sitting side by side on the sidewalk outside after having been "escorted" out. They were each halfway through their lecture at the historical society when they were grabbed where the pants hang loose and frog-marched to the door. And of course, the question that is then asked of the "heretic" is "Why do you associate with those lunatics out there on the sidewalk? Bad testimony. We have to do better. We have to seek the approval of those who run the guild." And they will always give it . . . but there are conditions.

But it is not enough simply to be contrarians. Should we strive for a *lack* of scholarship in what we do? Certainly not, because such anti-intellectualism has a bad case of its own besetting sins as well. Proud ignorance is no better than proud knowledge. The problem is the human heart, which is always just a few inches below the head, whether or not the head in question is full of axle grease or erudite learning. Why does Paul taunt the wise man, the scholar of the age? It was because with all his learning, he did not know God.

The fear of the Lord is the beginning of knowledge (Prov. 1:7). It may sound arrogant to say something like this, but it is genuine humility. "I have more insight than all my teachers, for I meditate on your statutes" (Ps. 119:99). One of the foundational prerequisites for faithful study in *any* area, including that of American history, is a fear of the Lord, and a complete willingness to ground everything on the Word of God. Only God is omniscient, and when we compare how much any human being knows (in his field) with how much there is to be known in that field, the only marvel is that any of us knows anything at all. How much history *is* there, and how much of it made it into the historical record? "What is man, that You are mindful of him?"

I.

Regenerate but Unreconstructed

Ash on an old man's sleeve
Is all the ash burnt roses leave.
Dust in the air suspended
Marks the place where a story ended.
                    from "Little Gidding"
                    T. S. Eliot

I MUST BEGIN with an apology. The title of this short essay is taken with a little twist from John Crowe Ransom's famous essay, his contribution to the collective defiance rendered to the ugliness of modernity by the Southern Agrarians in *I'll Take My Stand*. My apology is for explaining an allusion in such a heavy-handed way, but it is necessary because I am writing this essay as a result of controversy with some "professional historians," men who belong to a class of persons in which every important allusion is sure to be missed, or, if caught, misconstrued. But since this is written to explain, rather than obscure, the heavy-handedness must be endured. So what do I mean by *regenerate?* What do I mean by *unreconstructed?*

Ransom meant that the South should accept the encroachments of blighted industrialism as inevitable (reconstructed) but that the South should offer this acceptance with a bad grace (unregenerate): "The South at last is to be physically reconstructed; but it will be fatal if the South should conceive it as her duty to be regenerated."[1]

1. Twelve Southerners, *I'll Take My Stand: The South and the Agrarian Tradition* (Baton Rouge: Louisiana State Univ. Press, 1977 [1930]), 22.

While there is an important point here that is well worth articulating and defending, I am writing from much further downstream. The river of modernity is still flowing, and there is a lot more gunk in it than there was in 1930, along with a few more shopping carts half-buried in the weeds along the bank. But there is an additional element in all this as well. Way downstream as we are, we have a bit more perspective—and can perhaps identify at least some of the pollution in this particular river as the responsibility of the Old South. And that is why I would want to reverse his phrase to accommodate our changing circumstances—regenerate but unreconstructed. But this requires explanation.

In the fall of 2003, a controversy erupted in the small town where I live in northern Idaho. The controversy concerned a booklet I co-wrote with Steve Wilkins in the mid-nineties entitled *Southern Slavery as It Was.*[2] It was the contention of this booklet that the *way* in which slavery ended has had ongoing deleterious consequences for modern Christians in our current culture wars, and that slavery was far more benign in practice than it was made to appear in the literature of the abolitionists. We were *not* trying to maintain that slavery in itself was a positive good, like food, air, or sunlight. Our central interest was in defending the integrity and applicability of the Scriptures to our current cultural controversies, and we affirmed that Christians who apologize for what the Bible teaches on slavery will soon be apologizing for what it teaches on marriage. We wrote as Christian apologists, but not the kind who apologize for being Christians.

The relevance of our concerns was underscored this last year when the high court of Massachusetts imposed (in principle) homosexual marriages on the rest of the states through the full faith and credit clause of the Constitution. Somehow, I find it hard to believe that R. L. Dabney would have been surprised by any of this, either with the nature of the cul-de-sac error, or the commonwealth

2. Steve Wilkins and Douglas Wilson, *Southern Slavery as It Was* (Moscow: Canon Press, 1996). That booklet, now extensively revised, is a separate chapter in this book and shouldn't be too hard to find.

from which it came. We have not seen this level of moral folly in
high places since Caligula made his horse a senator.

Our particular controversy arose because the local newspaper
erroneously reported that we were holding a conference on the
subject of slavery, and it was not long before many of the local
leftists were screeching like so many progressive tea kettles. In the
course of the ensuing controversy, I found myself accused of many
amazing things, a number of which were as fully immoral as a
decision by the United States Supreme Court. Naturally, I felt I
needed to defend myself. Some accusations were slanderous, some
were confused, and some were just half a bubble off.

In this last category was the accusation that I am a neo-Confederate. This is close in one way, but at the same time it is not at all
accurate. The tag *neo-Confederate* conjures up images of a handful
of disillusioned yahoos setting up a tiny republic in a trailer park
east of Houston somewhere. But it must be admitted that a more
accurate name would require explanation as well. This is because
I am not a neo-Confederate; I am a *paleo*-Confederate. And with
this acknowledgment comes my need for a phrase like "regenerate
but unreconstructed."

You see my difficulty. The problem with such a phrase is not
what it actually means. The problem is that it is the kind of
phrase that semi-literate journalists *think* they understand. And
half-educated history professors react to it by maintaining that
I have no right to an opinion on paleo-anything—for I am not a
trained professional historian, with a doctorate on "the ingestion of
cough syrups in west London, 1815–1830, a study in contrasts."[3]

---

3. Lest I insult any reputable historians accidentally, the particular historians I have
in mind are Drs. Quinlan, Ramsey, and Graden, all in the employ of the University of
Idaho, the most accredited higher institution of learning north of Riggins, also in Idaho.
They are deeply concerned that my views on this entire subject pose a grave threat to
human rights. Meanwhile Dr. Quinlan teaches a course in which the students ingest the
porno-violence of the Marquis de Sade (even though Quinlan disapproves of de Sade),
and Dr. Graden is a cheerleader for Stalin and Ho Chi Minh. Perhaps their vigilance on
behalf of human rights could be exercised *(ahem)* in a more profitable direction.

But I have used the term *paleo-Confederate* anyway, for the honest reader will be honest enough to wonder what such a word could mean, and perhaps be curious enough to read a small essay on it. At the same time, it is important for me to emphasize that by using the term *paleo-Confederate* I do not wish to limit my historical allegiances to anything so provincially American, and so I would *also* want to identify myself as a paleo-medieval, a paleo-conservative, a paleo-Constantinian, a paleo-Puritan, a paleo-Chestertonian, and a paleo-spear Dane.

Regenerate

As a conservative Reformed minister, I affirm that God governs the world through covenant sanctions; He both blesses and curses. I take it as self-evident that in the disastrous outcome of the War Between the States, God was pouring out His wrath *upon the South*. Since our God is never capricious or arbitrary in His judgments, this outpouring of wrath was just and righteous in every respect.

Understanding the outcome of the war as a judgment from God was common among pious Southerners at the time. This understanding in no way vindicated the sins of the North, for God had once used the wickedness of Assyria to humiliate a backslidden Israel. Our sovereign God draws straight with crooked lines. This was a lesson that Habakkuk had to learn, and Dabney sorrowfully repeated the lesson: "A righteous God, for our sins towards Him, has permitted us to be overthrown by our enemies and His."[4]

A biblical view of the world makes a distinction between a wicked nation, an axe in the hand of God, and the holiness of the sovereign hand that wields it (Is. 10:5). This is why, when considering something as awful as Sherman's March to the Sea, we should be aghast at the wickedness of this form of warfare, and simultaneously we must recognize that as wielded by the hand of God, this judgment was not wickedness at all. It was not falling upon the South because

---

4. R. L. Dabney, *A Defense of Virginia and the South* (Harrisonburg.: Sprinkle Publications, 1977), 356.

of some few cultural peccadilloes or trifles. Whatever it was that caused God to bring such a judgment, it was a really big deal.

But confession of sin and repentance require that the sins be *named*. This involves more than acknowledging the mere fact of unnamed sin somewhere. It means that specific sins should be named. In *Southern Slavery as It Was*, we repudiated the racism that was often seen as justification for the system of slavery. The fact that racism was virtually universal, in both the North and South, does not serve as an adequate justification. Our standard must be Scripture, and never what is commonly practiced around us.

The reason we were attacked in our little controversy in Moscow was not because we would not condemn racism as a sin; we had done so repeatedly and clearly. The reason we were slandered in the way we were was simply because we refused to say that racism was a sin against the State or against humanity. All sin, if it is indeed sin, is sin *against* God. It is God's character and law which are offended by sin. We maintain that racism is a sin against God, and that it will be judged in the light of His holiness at the last day. It is not a sin against Congress or against the Supreme Court. It is not a sin against the whims of *demos* or against the bureaucrats down at Health and Human Services. God hates it, and He always will. But democrats do not want a final or ultimate word like this. Of course sins against God do harm and hurt individuals, and in this lesser sense, sins against God are also sins against the victim. But even here, when King David confessed his sin of murder and adultery, he says to God, "Against thee, thee only, have I sinned" (Ps. 51:4).

We are living in the Regeneration of the world, an eon brought about by the death, burial, and resurrection of Jesus Christ. Because of this, we answer to Him, and because we answer to Him, we condemn racism. The necessity of condemning racism is clearly revealed in Scripture, an acknowledged authority by many Southerners. Their racism was less virulent in a number of ways than what was found in the North, but it was more blameworthy. To whom much is given, much is required.

Both Northerners and Southerners were misled by the obvious inferiority of black *culture* at that time, which had nothing to do with whether blacks bore the image of God in man, and everything to do with whether the gospel had yet had an opportunity to do its work within black culture. There are few things funnier than watching Europeans and those of European descent look down their noses at primitive cultures, taking pride in themselves. But what do you have, St. Paul asks, that you did not receive as a gift? And if you received it as a gift, why do you boast as though you did not? What was Europe like before the gospel arrived *there?* The answer is that it was every bit as wretched as anything you might dredge up from the history of the fens of Africa. Not that many centuries ago, *my* ancestors were engaged in idolatry, human sacrifice, and mindless superstitions, and I have heard about some berserkers who would strip naked, paint themselves blue, and run into battle. Just a few centuries later, taking the long view, their descendants would be building cathedrals and writing symphonies. The gospel is the issue—grace, not race.

Anyone who would labor fruitfully in building the kingdom of God must understand this. Anyone who wants to learn what is valuable from the theology of the Southern theologians, political theorists, cultural writers, and so on (and there is a great deal to learn), must resolve to understand this as well. The kingdom of God is not tied to one nation, one ethnic tradition, or one stream of cultural development. Christ commanded us to preach the gospel to every creature. The universal salvation offered by Him means that all who turn in repentance away from their idolatries—whether African, aboriginal, American, or alternative—will be forgiven. Moreover, the prophets declare in many glorious passages that all the ends of the earth will turn, repent, and call upon the Lord. Their lives, families, households, tribes, and nations will be transformed by the power of the gospel. The Christian faith *is* the future of this world.[5] The wonderful result will be a Trinitarian glory

5. Philip Jenkins, *The Next Christendom* (Oxford: Oxford Univ. Press, 2002).

which will include lots of brown and tan, red and yellow, black and white.

Any political or theological conservatism that does not accept this, press for it, pray for it, and yearn for it is a conservatism that must be born again. "Thy kingdom come, thy will be done, *on earth as it is in heaven.*" This means that regeneration, in the sense I am speaking of here, must include rejection of every form of racial hatred, animosity or vainglory. In Christ there is neither Jew nor Greek, slave or free, male or female. But here is the difficulty—we know how to "reject" such forms of racism in our modern and sentimental way. We know how to throw racism off the egalitarian train. But how do we deal with this problem in Christendom? The Old South was a nation in that old order of Christendom, and they did *not* deal with it. Why didn't they? And if we learn from them on subjects like culture, order, hierarchy, honor, and agrarianism, will this mean that we (inevitably) must buy into racist assumptions? Certainly not, and working through these issues is one of the reasons for this book.

Unreconstructed

So I also take it as a given that the South was right on all the essential constitutional and cultural issues surrounding the war, and this is my reason for calling myself unreconstructed. I do not want to stick to my guns on this as a matter of pride, or because the issue is at the top of my list of priorities. It is not. But even so, I will not recant anything concerning that war, however trivial, simply because the current regime of *intoleristas* demands that I do so. Robert E. Lee is not at the center of my worldview or my theology. But when people start demanding that I treat him as an historical pariah, a peer in some way to Himmler, I am not going to do it. Lee was a gracious Christian gentleman, a brother in Christ, and an honorable man. Part of his greatness was his role in resisting the progress of the Revolution here in America.

The American Revolution was not a true revolution in the modern sense of that word, but the French Revolution *was* such a true

revolution. This does not exhaust the subject. The fact that the
American Revolution was not part of *the* Revolution does not mean
that we have not gone through our own Revolution, one that cor-
responds to that of France. We *have* experienced our equivalent
of the French Revolution, and it was a revolution that ended at
Appomattox: "Nor can we rely upon any evidence from the United
States of America. The real revolution in that country was not what
is called the Revolution in the history books, but is a consequence
of the Civil War."[6]

The nineteenth century was the century for revolutions, even if
we allow for the French Revolution in the last decade of the eigh-
teenth century and the Russian Revolution in the first decades of
the twentieth. The War Between the States was our participation
in those widespread global upheavals. The Revolution, generically
considered, is an enemy of the Christian faith, and it is an enemy
that has not gone away. The effect and the influence of it surround
us daily. Although some of the new currents were involved in it, the
American War for Independence was fundamentally a conservative
movement in defense of the old order. The Civil War was not; that
conflagration transformed our nation in much the same way that
the French Revolution transformed France.

But our concern in all this is not to go back and try to undo the
French Revolution or fight the battle of Gettysburg all over again.
Our central concern (and in some ways, our only concern) is to
be faithful Christians *now*. And we cannot be faithful Christians
now if we try to build the kingdom of God on shaky or rotten
foundations. The new wine of the gospel will necessarily burst the
Enlightenment wineskins. And yet, most contemporary Christians
have turned their wine into grape juice in order to prevent the
wineskins from coming to such an unhappy end.

The culture wars we are currently engaged in are real and con-
sequential, but those on the "traditional values" side of the conflict
are consistently outmaneuvered because they refuse to go back to

---

6. T. S. Eliot, *Christianity and Culture* (New York: Harcourt Brace, 1948), 118.

first principles. They do not see that unless Christ is acknowledged as Lord in the public square (but first in the church and home), then every manner of rebellion and disobedience must be tolerated there. Given that Christ is our only possible Savior, how is it that Christians believe that Christ can be banished from our public life, while simultaneously believing that sin and disobedience can be kept out of our public life by some other means, some other savior? How can we reject Christ in this way and *not* have homosexual marriage?

This has happened because Christians have allowed themselves to be maneuvered into accepting the tag of "right wing." But the terms *left wing* and *right wing* come from the seating of the revolutionary legislature in France *following* the Revolution. Those seated on the right were the moderate revolutionaries. Those on the left were the fire eaters, the radicals. And this is why the Revolution continues on, not resisted by many consistent voices at all. The car of the Revolution is barreling down the highway, and a few traditional-values conservatives have got a back door open and are trying to slow the thing down by dragging their feet on the pavement. It does not appear to be working. Virtually all conservatives accept the *fact* of the car and the *fact* of the highway. The only thing they dispute anymore is the speed. Groen van Prinsterer put it well when he said, "Conservatism, without a Christian-historical basis, is the inconsistent wing of liberalism."[7] And those inconsistencies will eventually work their way out into the light of day. R. L. Dabney made the same point when referring to a certain species of conservatism:

> American conservatism is merely the shadow that follows Radicalism as it moves forward toward perdition. . . . It is worthless because it is the conservatism of expediency only, and not of sturdy principle. It intends to risk nothing serious for the sake of the truth, and has no idea of being guilty of the folly of martyrdom.[8]

---

7. Groen van Prinsterer, *Lectures on Unbelief and Revolution* (Jordan Station: Wedge Publishing Foundation, 1989), fn. 425.

8. R. L. Dabney, *Discussions, Vol. 4: Secular* (Harrisonburg: Sprinkle Publications, 1979), 496.

One wag has commented that if the Democrats suggested a plan to burn down the Capitol building, the Republicans would counter with a plan to do it over the course of three years. Our nation's leftists want to drive the car over the cliff at 100 mph. Republicans want to go 50 mph.

This is why it is important for us to know what needs to stay unreconstructed and what must submit to the agony of the new birth. This unreconstructed worldview has to deal with culture, egalitarianism, constitutional interpretation, and fundamentally with race and slavery. Eugene Genovese makes an important comment in this respect in a review of a book by Clyde Wilson:

> But Wilson, like his fellow southern conservatives, pays dearly for his philosophical idealism. Hostile to slavery and racism, he seeks to root the positive qualities he finds in the life of the Old South in an older Christian civilization and transatlantic republicanism. Too good a historian to treat slavery as a bagatelle, he nonetheless underestimates its effect on the formation of southern culture, ideals, and character.[9]

This is the dilemma for the one who would be unreconstructed. I don't want to underestimate the effects of slavery on the South or minimize any enormities. As Genovese said, slavery was no bagatelle. But neither do I want to ignore the biblical teaching on slavery and act as though the Christian defenders of antebellum slavery had no clue what the Scriptures said about this. They knew the apostolic instructions precisely, had their exegesis in hand, and consistently bested the abolitionists in debate.

All of this means that the areas that need to remain unreconstructed and the areas that must be regenerate are not discrete, but rather overlap. If we are to recover our fathers' wisdom, and stay free of their faults, we will have to follow the instruction of St. Peter, and gird up the loins of our minds.

9. Eugene Genovese, *The Southern Front: History and Politics in the Cultural War* (Columbia: Univ. of Missouri Press, 1995), 30.

2.

Black and Tan

I FIRST SWAM into reflective consciousness in Annapolis, Maryland, a segregated city, in the late fifties and early sixties. A few years later, this was juxtaposed with a very different racial experience in my high school years in Ann Arbor, Michigan, and that strange juxtaposition provides the backdrop for some modest observations on race relations in America.

In Annapolis, I attended the elementary school for white children (Germantown Elementary) that was a mile or so from our house. Adam's Park Elementary, the black elementary school, was just down the block. As children do, I just took these things in stride; this was just the way the world was. When the results of the Supreme Court integration decision finally filtered down to Annapolis, my father was instrumental in redrawing some of the lines on the map, and I was sent to the middle school (that had previously been the black high school), and my younger sister went to Adam's Park. She was one of a tiny handful of white kids in her school. When my youngest brother went to kindergarten there, his famous comment was, "I'm the only kid with a face like mine." This experiment in social engineering, ordered from on high, did not initially go that well, for many of the white families in town betook themselves to the private "white flight" academies. My father didn't want to have anything to do with segregation, so I went to an integrated (and tense) middle school, and my sister was vastly outnumbered. I recall that she got roughed up when Martin Luther King, Jr. was shot.

We moved to Ann Arbor in 1968, just in time for the heyday of radicalism there. My high school had an SDS chapter (Students for a Democratic Society, a group of crazies from the sixties), and one day I was surprised, coming out of my homeroom class, to see a line of cops run by with their billy clubs at the ready. Apparently a race riot of some sort was in progress, and I walked around to the front of the school to discover that an attorney/spokesman for the rioters was already there on the front steps, holding forth to the reporters. It was an agitprop event, and the grievances were being aired in a *very* professional way.

Because Ann Arbor was a liberalism-on-steroids kind of place, it was soon decided that our high school needed to have a town meeting of some sort, with students of representative races meeting on a panel, and we could all talk our way into racial harmony. For some reason, I was selected to be a white kid on the panel. I remember a few things about that evening; indeed it would be hard *not* to remember them. One of my co-panelists was aggrieved over the book *Little Black Sambo*. But Sambo was not an African-American; he was from the subcontinent. And besides, as I recall saying that evening, I had nothing but the highest respect for Sambo. If anyone asked me to turn tigers into butter for *my* pancakes, I confess that I would be entirely nonplussed.

But the highlight of the evening was the moderator of the panel, a black media celebrity of sorts from the Detroit big time. He didn't do a very good job of moderating, and finally intruded himself into the discussion in quite a remarkable way. The Q & A time was approaching, and this gentleman (whose name escapes me) delivered an encyclical bull that notified all of us that in the history of the world, the only race that had *ever* been guilty of racism was the white race, and that the only recipient of said racism had been the black race. My father, who was in the audience, is an amateur military historian, and when called on, proceeded to give the rest of us a long (but by no means exhaustive) list of all the ethnic groups that he could think of that hated other ethnic groups, for no good reason. This intrusion of historical facts into a meeting that was going swimmingly without them was of course conveniently overlooked, the meeting finally ended, and nothing was fixed.

My father had taught me, both in Maryland and in Michigan, that not only does the truth matter, but without the Scriptures, we have no access to the truth of God. When Scripture is ignored, *all* our truths get relativized and soon cease to be truths at all. The center does not hold, and when we look around, we find that we are in the midst of a riot of postmodern hooey issuing forth from the academy. But the truth matters anyway, regardless of how many people come to view it as elastic. Because of this, our family had nothing to do with the white racism we had to deal with around us in Annapolis. I had boyhood friends who were black, and when they came over to our house to play, our neighbor lady (a sweet widow, really) let us know that she did not welcome my friends going onto her lawn. It was fine for us to do that, but not them. A young man boarded with our family one year, and I remember him leaving a hamburger joint downtown when they refused to let a black customer sit down inside after he had purchased his lunch. So our friend went outside with him, and they had lunch together sitting on the curb. All of this I internalized, storing the lessons up.

Because God's truth matters, we recognized the black reactions in Ann Arbor as manifest follies. But if you are critical of an approved victim class, you must be "racist." We saw white folly in Annapolis and black folly in Ann Arbor. And I stored all these examples up as well. It struck me for the first time (but not for the last) that it was odd how the same family could be considered "nigger-lovers" in Maryland and racists in Michigan. Latitude and longitude can apparently do quite a lot. But the reason for this Christian refusal to "stay put in our pigeon-hole" is not hard to figure out and brings us to the point of this essay.

Shared Dignity in Adam

Blacks and whites (and all other children of Adam) are created in the image of God, and as image-bearers all human beings are to be treated with dignity and respect. Scripture makes this very plain in multiple ways, and we have no basis for ranking the races in any way (with regard to the *imago Dei*) that privileges one above the other. A black man bears the image of God in just the same way that a white man does—no gradations permitted.

God created the human race in Adam and Eve, and all of us are descended from them, and are therefore cousins. Lest the point be missed, we are also all descended from Noah and his wife (again), and it turns out we are *still* cousins. Racial vanity and racial animosity can find no foundation in Scripture.

> And they sung a new song, saying, Thou are worthy to take the book, and to open the seals thereof: for thou wast slain, and hast redeemed us to God by thy blood out of every kindred, and tongue, and people and nation; and hast made us unto our God kings and priests: and we shall reign on the earth. (Rev. 5: 9–10)

John's vision not only says that Christ's blood is available to forgive all sinners from every part of the human race, but he also says that these individuals are more than forgiven—they are made kings and priests, and they shall reign on the earth. Enslaved blacks in the antebellum South who came to faith in Christ were coming to something far greater than personal forgiveness. Where the Spirit of the Lord is, there is liberty, and when Christ brings men to salvation, He also brings them (over time) into cultural maturity. There is no biblical reason for assuming that any race of men will be shortchanged in this. What possible exegetical grounds could we have for saying that blacks can be forgiven, but are somehow excluded from enjoying the fruits of cultural maturity? This is important because paternalistic Christian whites have sometimes allowed blacks into the faith because they have no trouble seeing how blacks need forgiveness. But the astounding grace of the gospel never stops with just forgiveness; the forgiven one is always summoned to glory. And not an invisible Gnostic glory either.

> And have put on the new man, which is renewed in knowledge after the image of him that created him: where there is neither Greek nor

Jew, circumcision nor uncircumcision, Barbarian, Scythian, bond nor free: but Christ is all, and in all. (Col. 3:11)

The Scythians (referred to above) were crazy, about as bad as the northern Europeans were. Herodotus tells us how they used to flay their enemies and stretch the skins on a rack that was mounted on the back of their saddles. And *these* were a people, with a history like that, to be included in the new man, the renewed image of God in Christ.

> For as many of you as have been baptized into Christ have put on Christ. There is neither Jew nor Greek, there is neither bond nor free, there is neither male nor female: for yet are all one in Christ Jesus. And if ye be Christ's, then are ye Abraham's seed, and heirs according to the promise. (Gal. 3:27–29)

Christian baptism marks an individual as an heir of Abraham, who was promised the world (Rom. 4:13). That world was promised to Abraham and his seed, and that seed includes all those who are in Christ. The New Testament tells us over and over again, in the bluntest possible way, that no tribe is excluded, and that everyone who is brought into Christ is profoundly included in the eschatological glory that is coming. This does not eradicate social roles and cultural standards, but they are all put squarely in their place. Everyone in the faith is called to remember that "slave and free" are not categories that will be operative in the *eschaton*, and they are unlikely to be operative in Christian cultures where the gospel has significantly accomplished its work. The fact that many Christians have failed to recognize this should not surprise us. Christians fail at a lot of things, but the Scriptures continue to summon us back.

This background provides the general context for the many incidental references in Scripture to racial harmony. But this harmony (figured so powerfully at Pentecost, a reversal of Babel) is *only possible in Christ*, as a result of the leaven of the gospel being introduced. Christopher Dawson once commented that the Christian church lives in the light of eternity and can afford to be patient. This *patience* is why St. Paul could tell slaves to obey their masters, even when the masters were fellow Christians (I Tim. 6:1–2). The leaven *will* do its work; in the meantime, we know where we are going, and we know (if we believe our Bibles), that all races in Christ are going there together.

The church at Antioch had an integrated leadership, presuming we know the reason for Simeon's nickname (Acts 13:1). Moses married a black woman from Cush (Num. 12:1). But those who are racially persnickety sometimes point to Acts 17:26, where St. Paul says that God "hath made of one blood all nations of men for to dwell on all the face of the earth, and hath determined the times before appointed, and the bounds of their habitation." "Ah," they say. "The bounds of their habitation must necessarily refer to the other side of the tracks. God *wants* us to stay apart." But this use of the passage misses the point completely. God is sovereign, and *He* determines how all the various nations of the earth live, mix, mingle, assimilate, or whatever else they do. God is sovereign over all of it. This is God's decretive will, which involves believers and unbelievers equally, whether Kurds, Hittites, Scots-Irish, or Zulus. This decretive will can include scattering or assimilation, extinction or absorption, apartheid or integration—it refers to *whatever* happens in history. God is always sovereign and He remains sinless even when He is perfectly controlling sin. But God's preceptive will (what He requires of His people in covenant with Him), summons us to a vision of the Church which is gloriously international. This is not a Johnny-come-lately liberal vision with a Christian vocabulary sprinkled on top. The ethnic tensions between Jews and Gentiles, and their resolution in Christ, are what a good portion of the New Testament is *about*. The Christian church has been dealing with these issues (with varying degrees of success) for two millennia.

Shared Sinfulness in Adam

But the next point is necessary also. As children of Adam, blacks and whites together are all *sinners*. This means that when it comes to the righteous judgments of God, no one of any race is in a position to exempt members of his own race from that judgment. No one is righteous, not even one.

All attempts to make the white mistreatment of blacks in America into a unique event in the history of the world are actually attempts to say (surreptitiously) that since this sin is unique, the redemption that we bring to it must also be unique. Jesus may have died on the cross for *ordinary* sins, such as lying, sleeping in the wrong bed, or cheating on crossword puzzles, but since this sin is unique in the history of the world, it calls for more, something else—reparations, perpetual liberal guilt, something big and done by us. And when I say "done by us," I mean by the appropriate federal agency.

But racism and slavery and mistreatment and genocide are *not* unique. This is how fallen and rebellious human beings treat one another. The Serbs did it to the Croats, the Germans did it to the Jews, the Idahoans did it to the Nez Perce, the Turks did it to the Armenians, the Iraqis did it to the Kurds. . . . I trust you get the general drift. This is what life outside of Christ is normally like— red and yellow, black and white—and even when the gospel of Christ comes to a people, it can often take centuries to get them to knock off some of their more resilient pagan practices. For example, how long did it take Europeans to get rid of polygamy? And at the headwaters of the slave trade to America there were blacks going to war with other blacks, enslaving their brothers, taking them down to the coast, and selling them.

The Son of God did not come to earth in order to deal with our petty foibles. The Incarnation was not brought on because we had been filching too many paper clips. The slaughter of the innocents at Bethlehem is just as much part of the Christmas story as the angels and the shepherds, and it reminds us of the enormities that Christ came to save us from. And there has been much to forgive, much to remove, on every continent and from every tribe. None of us is clean in himself. So do whites need to seek and receive forgiveness for their treatment of the black man? Absolutely. But blacks also need the cleansing blood of Christ—some of it for treatment of fellow blacks, some for responding to white hatred with hatred, some of it for taking mistreatment of a great-grandfather as a license for crime, and so on. We are, all of us, sinners. And it is not fitting for a sinner to look sideways at someone else and say, "Well, I'm less of a sinner than you."

Apart from grace, there is no such thing as moral superiority. No individual, no tribe, no nation, can say that they have achieved righteousness. Righteousness is a gift of God, and when it is given, the result is a genuine moral superiority—but that change was a *gift*, and the recipients know it to be a gift. As soon as the recipients forget this crucial point, that is clear evidence that they have lost the gift.

Secularist Inconsistencies

The philosopher David Stove objects to the use of the phrase "racial prejudice" because it brings with it an implied soteriology, and his point is well taken. In its place, he thinks we ought to use the phrase "racial animosity":

> Accordingly, when we call racial antagonism "racial prejudice," we imply that the antagonism depends on some false or irrational belief about the other race. Now, this is a distinctly *cheering* thing to imply. For we all know that it is possible for false or irrational beliefs to be corrected. That, after all, is one of the very things that *education* exists for, and which it often achieves. Here, then, is the secret attraction of the phrase "racial prejudice": it cheers us all up, by suggesting—as "racial antagonism," for example, does *not* suggest—that it is within the power of education to remove racial antagonism.[1]

If man is basically good, as secularists like to claim, then why does he do evil? The typical humanist answer, going back at least to Socrates, is that man (who is basically good) does evil because he is ignorant. But if evil is caused by ignorance, then education must be a savior. Thus, something like racial *prejudice* can be addressed in the

1. David Stove, *Against the Idols of the Age* (London: Transaction Publishers, 1999), 139.

curriculum! But if we call it racial *animosity*, that sounds like a much more old-fashioned sin—the kind that Jesus has to forgive.

But the secularists persist in trying to fix the general cussedness of sinners by means of bromides and platitudes. Put human rights into our curricula, applaud sitcoms like *The Cosby Show*, buy the world a Coke, and soon everyone will come around for a great, big, cultural group hug. But they *don't* come around because animosity is the problem, not ignorance; and animosity is a question of the heart. Only Christ can change the heart.

At the same time, there is a deeper problem within the secularist worldview, one that all the bromides in the world cannot fix. By rejecting the biblical account of the origins of man (consequently rejecting the true *nature* of man) and accepting the evolutionary account as unquestionably true, the modern secularist state is ir-remediably committed to racist principles, whether they want to be or not. Fundamentalist Christians, even the ones who are openly (and unbiblically) bigoted against members of other races, are com-mitted (ultimately, in their *first* principles) to racial reconciliation—whether they like it or not.

In the nineteenth century when Darwin first made his appear-ance, no one had any problem with the racist implications of his theory. It was openly avowed and in fact was used as evidence. Before Darwin, secularist thinkers had advanced the idea of *poly-genesis*, the view that blacks and whites belonged to separate species entirely. Southern Christians like J. H. Thornwell and R. L. Dab-ney (who were defenders of slavery) hated this corruption of biblical truth, even though they shared the belief that blacks were inferior. Nevertheless, blacks were believed to be inferior *men*, descendants of Adam, and fellow heirs of the salvation offered by Christ. The "progressives," wide open to whatever science might say, had no trouble saying that blacks were another entity entirely. Genovese makes this observation:

> Thornwell praised the steadfast refusal of Southerners to em-
> brace polygenesis and scientific racism in their struggle against

abolitionism. A decade later he returned to the theme in Columbia, South Carolina: "No Christian man, therefore, can give any countenance to speculations which trace the negro to any other parent but Adam." He denounced the scientific racists as infidels.[2]

When Darwin offered the mechanism of natural selection to account for evolution, the logic of an unbelieving scientific racism became increasingly clear. If one species can be transformed into another, and if this is how we are to account for all the species we see around us, then what possible reason could we have for saying that once *homo sapiens* has "arrived," all evolutionary developments after that point must advance in lockstep, thus insuring that one branch of the human family will *never* be allowed to outstrip the others? Of course, there is no such reason, and Darwinists almost universally assumed that whites were further up the evolutionary tree than blacks.[3] If you grant the faulty premise, this makes perfect logical sense. Given evolution, and given variation within the human race, the most natural question in the world is which branch is the tallest.

This was a central characteristic of progressive thought in the nineteenth century and the first part of the twentieth. From Darwin, who provided the scientific rationale for such racism, to Margaret Sanger and her "human weeds," to George Bernard Shaw and the eugenics craze, to Hitler's final solution, progressives have a lot to answer for. But instead of answering for it, they dropped the whole thing like a hot rock after Hitler, and (of course) turned on traditionalist whites in the South who did not have the kind of flexibility in their joints that makes secularist advances in ethical theory so fun to watch. After a century or so of bloodshed and general mayhem in the name of progressivism, it was apparently time to upbraid Southern Christians for their intolerance.

2. Eugene Genovese, *A Consuming Fire* (Athens: Univ. of Georgia Press, 1998), 83.

3. This assumes that there is such a thing as "progress" in this scheme, but that is a problem with evolution generally. Strictly speaking, there is no such thing as progress in this system, but evolutionists cannot function without it. Otherwise, all we have is one Grand Evolutionary Meander, and how could we extract a "progressive" agenda from that?

In calling the Christian Church to a more scriptural commitment to racial harmony in Christ, this brief critique of evolutionary secularism is included because Christians need to repent before *God*. We need to seek forgiveness, but we do *not* need to seek it from those who have been the chief fomenters of discord for the last one hundred and fifty times around the sun.

Cultural Superiority

One of the things that racial harmony propaganda has done for us is make us think that racism never has any raw material to work with. In other words, we reduce the whole question to one of "star-bellied sneetches" and scratch our heads in amazement that intelligent people once thought that whites were superior to blacks. Of course we know they were wrong for thinking this, but they were not *stupid* in thinking this. They were dealing with objective facts, which (they assumed) could only have one explanation. It was this latter assumption that tripped them up so badly, and not the objective realities they were trying to account for.

Picture a kid in the seventh grade looking down on those woefully benighted fifth-graders. His knowledge is vaster, his sophistication sleeker, his skateboard wider, his pride complete. Now think of Europeans and Africans.

In reaction to the legacy of racism that has long been directed toward blacks, many liberals have adopted the emotionally secure (but intellectually indefensible) position of egalitarianism, the view that equality in the sight of God means sameness in the sight of man. This is the facts-be-damned approach. But there is no effective way to address racial hatreds by insisting that everyone (all together now) start denying the obvious. All men exhibit the image of God equally, but all cultures are *not* equal. As we look at all the tribes of men, we see some that have landed a man on the moon, and some that have not yet worked out the concept of the wheel. We have some with one whole row in the supermarket dedicated to shampoo, while in another tribe hair is washed in cow urine. We have orchestras playing *The Brandenburg Concertos* compared to someone beating on a hollow log with a couple of sticks. Now I am fully aware that to assert the superiority of one culture over another is enough to convict me of the charge of racism (as it is currently defined) in the minds of many. And I grant that it is quite possible that someone *could* argue for cultural superiority as a coded way of asserting the innate superiority of those individuals (and their genes!) who make up that superior culture.

But while some may have done this, it is not at all what I am doing here. For those who do not want to listen to the argument, I have nothing more to say. For some, the mere denial of egalitarianism is enough to brand one as a racist forever, and since I am interested in taunting egalitarianism every chance I get, I have little hope of gaining their favor. But the root of my denial of egalitarianism is my belief in the superiority of the grace of God over and against every form of human works. The only true antithesis is between the seed of the woman and the seed of the serpent. The Christian faith *is* "superior" (being true and all), and so it brings blessings with it.

It is a fact that there is a wide disparity (of refinement and achievement) between cultures. One problem that results from this disparity, according to a Christian worldview, is that those who embrace this fact tend to attribute it to their own innate worth. They give the whole thing a false cause. And those who would deny *that* particular folly do so by embracing another, which is to deny that there is any disparity worth mentioning.

But there are such disparities, and they are present because of the uneven progress of the gospel throughout the world. Everything that we enjoy culturally is simply the grace of God. What do we of "the West" have that we did not receive as a gift? And if as a gift, then why do we boast as though it were not a gift (I Cor. 4:7)? Before the gospel came to my ancestors, what were we whites (with our alleged *soo*-perior genetics) doing with ourselves? Well, we were painting ourselves blue and running naked into battle. We would undergo warp spasms in order to fight in a completely gonzo condition. We were living in huts with thatched roofs and cooking our food over animal dung. If I were offered a pot of that food today, the chances are pretty good that I would not be interested in eating it. We routinely conducted human sacrifice. We would capture Roman engines of warfare and be completely clueless about how to operate them. In a short word, we were barbarians, savages. So what transformed northern Europe, which was every bit as dark as the worst you might dig up in Africa's history? The answer is the preaching of the gospel of Jesus Christ, crucified and risen. As the Christian faith transformed Europe (and the loss of it is deforming it back again), so the Christian faith is in the process of transforming Africa. As a postmillennialist, I look forward to the time when the cathedrals, symphonies, and literature of Africa will put to shame the current achievements of dead white guys—not to take anything away from *them*, but there is a lot past seventh grade awaiting all human cultures in Christ. So white supremacists are like that kid in seventh grade, absolutizing the present moment for all the wrong reasons.

This brings up another point: why is it that the "supremacists" among us behave the way they do? If there is a kid in seventh grade who is busy heaping contempt upon the heads of the fifth-graders, it is likely that he is not exactly the class genius. He is struggling to fulfill his duties, and quickly finds that it is easier to puff himself up by looking down on someone a couple grades down the hall than it is to actually do his own work. In short, if the case for white supremacy *had* to be made (for some absurd reason), the people that would be picked to *make* that case would not be your rank and file white supremacist. Blacks and whites who are blessed with any genuine superiority (of any kind) should know it to be a gift. And if they believe their Bibles, they hold that the same kind of gift is coming to the whole world.

Black and Tan

The image is taken from a great mixture of beers—or if you like, miscegenated beer.[4] Many consider the classic black and tan to be

---

4. And no, the "black and tan" is not being used here as a metaphor for segregation, and neither is it being used to urge intermarriage as a moral imperative, although that is certainly lawful. It is a metaphor for dwelling together in harmony, in Christ.

a mixture of Bass Pale Ale and Guinness, which actually sounds worthwhile. Black and tan in a larger sense refers to the relationship of the black race and the white race here in America. What are we to do? Where do we go from here?

Apart from Christ, the answer is that we cannot go anywhere. We cannot do anything but sit around and wait for the tensions to rise. In Christ, and only there, can dark and light beer go together. There are many compelling reasons why the lordship of Jesus Christ must be acknowledged in the American public square (e.g., homosexual marriage, abortion, etc.), but race relations should be near the top of the list. Racial animosity is a public fact. Racial hostility has public consequences. The state is helpless in trying to deal with this kind of thing, and when the state has adopted the tenets of secularism, the situation gets markedly worse. Why is *anything* good or bad? By what standard are we seeking to accomplish anything?

Those liberals who are sincerely distressed at the increased coarsening of our public life need to be invited, as by an old-time hedge preacher or hot-gospeler, to "come to Jesus." It is never enough to tell people simply to "be nice." They have no reason to, and they don't want to. Men and women are sinners and they need salvation, not lessons in etiquette. The messianic State doesn't have any salvation to give. Apart from Christ, we *can* accomplish hatred, anarchy, and balkanization. Leave it to us. But if we want an intact civilization, if we want a place where we can sit down in a pub and order a black and tan, we need Jesus Christ. In the forties and fifties, there were jazz clubs called "black and tans," but such rapprochements are only temporary, needing a stronger glue than jazz. All cultures must have a *cultus* at the center, and as a Christian I think it only right that the Christian *cultus* should occupy that place. The Christian faith, being true, is the only faith that can bring about true and complete racial reconciliation. Right next to the public square, we need to look up and see a church spire, a place where the Bible is believed and preached, where the Word and sacraments are offered together, and offered to a black and tan congregation.

3.

Scripture and Slavery

CHRISTIANS NEED TO understand this issue in order to remain faithful to the teaching of Scripture. By seeing how obedience to Scripture could quite possibly have protected our fathers (both Northern and Southern) from a costly and bloody war, had they only obeyed, we may be assured of the importance of submitting to the Scriptures when it comes to *our* controversies (e.g., militant feminism, homosexuality), no matter what the unbelieving world has to say about it.

The Slave Trade

The slave trade was an abomination, and those evangelicals in England like William Wilberforce who led the fight against it are rightly considered heroes of the faith. The Bible clearly rejects the practice of slave trading (1 Tim. 1:10; Exod. 21:16). In a just social order, slave trading could rightly be punished with death.

Slavery in the Bible

In considering slavery itself, we must recognize the difference between slavery regulated by the Mosaic law—that is, a slavery which was little more than an indentured servanthood (bond apprenticeship for a time)—and slavery as it existed in a pagan empire such as Rome. In ancient Israel, it was the duty of those who feared God to simply obey the laws concerning slavery as God had given them, recognizing their temporary nature. The laws on slavery in the Old Testament begin with manumission or release from slavery in view (Exod. 21:2) and were given to a people who themselves had just been freed from bondage in Egypt (Exod. 20:1–2). The temporary nature of Hebraic slavery was built into it as a design feature.

But when the existing law was that of an unbelieving pagan order, like that of Rome, it was the duty of Christians living within that system to follow the biblical instructions for resisting the paganism of this slavery *carefully* so that the Word of God would not be blasphemed (1 Tim. 6:1).

The distinction to be made here is between slavery that was regulated directly by God, which is what we see in the Old Testament among the Hebrews, and slavery that was instituted by an unbelieving and pagan world, which was therefore to be subverted by faithful Christians living in accordance with the gospel.

Racism

American slavery had the additional complication of its racial basis. And so we as Christians, and especially as American Christians, must denounce as a matter of biblical principle every form of racism, racial animosity, or racial vainglory. God created man in His own image and has made from one blood all the nations of the earth (Acts 17:26). We are called to believe firmly that in the gospel God has reversed the curse of Babel, and that in Christ there is neither Jew nor Greek, male or female, slave or free (Gal. 3:28), black or white, Asian or Hispanic, tall or short. Jesus Christ has purchased men from every nation and tribe with His own blood, and His blood necessarily provides a stronger bond than ours does.

Slavery as an Institution

Christ died on the cross to set all men free from their sins, and all forms of external and physical slavery are built on the bedrock of slavery to sin. Therefore, the logic of the Great Commission requires the eventual death of slavery as an institution in any place where it might still exist. While Christian slaves were commanded to work hard for their masters, Christian slaves were also told to take any lawful opportunity for freedom (1 Cor. 7:20–24). This indicates that slavery as an institution is inconsistent with the fundamental Spirit of the gospel, who is the Spirit of liberty (2 Cor. 3:17).

Godly Subversion of Slavery

The best way to subvert a pagan system of slavery is through careful obedience to the law of Christ. This means that while obedient Christians could have found themselves either slaves or masters, the instructions given to them in their respective stations are very clear. Christian masters were to remember that they had a Master in heaven, and this meant they had to treat their slaves charitably (Eph. 6:9). Christian slaves had to work diligently for their masters, knowing that ultimately they were doing their work for God and not for men (Eph. 6:5; Col. 3:22–23). And Christian slaves who happened to be owned by Christian masters were told to pay even *greater* attention to this submissive demeanor, because the beneficiary of their labors was a brother in Christ (1 Tim. 6:2; Phil. 10–19). These scriptural instructions, carefully followed, resulted, over time, in a peaceful elimination of Roman slavery, and had they been consistently applied by Southerners, they would have had an analogous impact on the slavery of the antebellum South.

Reformation or War?

The godly pattern of social renewal is never bloodthirsty. The radical insists on immediate action, through coercive, bloody, and political means. In contrast, the work of the gospel is done as silently as yeast working through the loaf, and the end result is liberation from sin, love for God, and love for one's neighbor. This love for neighbor necessitates the recognition that in Christ there is neither Jew nor Greek, slave nor free, male nor female, white nor black (Gal. 3:28). But those radicals who are impatient in their spirits always refuse God's teaching in such matters. They are proud and ignorant, loving verbal strife, envy, railing, and perverse disputes (1 Tim. 6:3–5). We speak for peace, but they are for war (Ps. 120:7).

4.

Southern Slavery and Our Culture Wars

THE SOUTH HAS long carried the stigma of racism and bigotry. The fact that slavery ended abruptly because the South lost the war serves to reinforce this common stereotype. For this reason, most Southerners take little pride (or the wrong kind of pride) in their nation's role in the War Between the States. The only thing they can boast about is how well they fought—but they are not allowed to defend the cause itself. They have been told that they cannot talk of principle or speak of righteousness. The institution of slavery has so tarnished the Southern position that nothing about the South can be viewed as good or right. Slavery is considered to be such a wicked practice that it alone is sufficient to answer the question of which side was right in that unfortunate war. The fact that the South practiced slavery is enough to cause many moderns to feel they do not even have to listen to the various biblical and constitutional arguments that swirled around that controversy. Consequently, to have a closed mind on this issue is to cloak oneself in virtue.[1]

How could intelligent men have supported slavery? The question is especially difficult when we consider that these were men who

1. A larger version of this essay appeared as *Southern Slavery as It Was*. This is about half the original length, and the atrocious errors that were found in the footnoting of that booklet have been removed. The original booklet was by Steve Wilkins and Douglas Wilson; in this current form the sections by Wilkins have been removed, although some of his contributions may still remain.

lived in a pervasively Christian culture. We have all heard of the heartlessness—the brutalities, immoralities, and cruelties—that were supposedly inherent and widespread in the system of slavery. We have heard of how slave families were broken up, of the rape of slave women, of the frequent brutal beatings, of the horrible living conditions, and of the unrelenting work schedule and back-breaking routine—all of which go together to form our impression of the crushing oppression which was slavery in the South. The truthfulness of this description has seldom been challenged.

One goal of this small essay is to show that if this impression is largely false, then the instructions laid down in the New Testament for Christians in slave-holding societies were applicable straight across—and those instructions did not include a war which would kill over 600,000 men. And conversely, if the New Testament instructions are considered authoritative, then we may be justified in concluding that many of the lurid pictures that have been painted about the South by abolitionists were less than accurate.

It is important to note at the outset, however, that this impression inherited from the abolitionists is not *entirely* false. The truth is, Southern slavery was open to sharp criticism (and more than this, open to *severe* judgment from God) because it did not follow the teaching of Scripture the way it should have. Some of the state laws regulating slavery were indefensible biblically (the laws forbidding the teaching of reading and writing, for example). One cannot defend the abuse some slaves had to endure. None can excuse the immorality some masters and overseers indulged in with some slave women. The separation of families that sometimes occurred was deplorable. These were sad realities in the Southern system, and when God finally determined to judge it, I am determined to say *amen* to the judgment. My purpose here is *not* to defend any such practices—where and when they occurred. I have no interest in defending the racism (in both the North and the South) which was often seen as the basic justification for the system, and I do in fact condemn it most heartily.[2]

2. For more on a biblical understanding of racism, please see the essay entitled "Black and Tan" elsewhere in this volume.

My concern is to lay out certain biblical principles and then draw broad conclusions from them. My purpose is not to provide a complete, detailed representation of the nature of Southern slavery; such a complete and accurate account has yet to be widely disseminated. As a consequence, there has been a great deal of falsehood paraded about in the pretense of truth. The South has been stigmatized and slandered, and generations have been misled over the true nature of the "peculiar institution" and, as a consequence, they have not understood the true nature of the South in general. We must know more of the truth about slavery. We have no concern to minimize the sins of the South—or the North, for that matter. Where there is sin, let us freely confess and forsake it. But because we have resolved to abandon sin, *this must include the sin of believing a lie.*[3]

So Why Write About *This?*

In the mid-seventies, American evangelicals began to wake up to the fact that our culture was beginning to tumble down around our ears. In 1973 the Supreme Court ruled that it was unconstitutional for the various states to outlaw the dismemberment of the unborn. Men like Francis Schaeffer were used by God to rattle the pervasive evangelical complacency and to make us realize the ramifications of what was occurring—and what was coming.

So a significant minority of the evangelical church began to mobilize and plunged into a cultural war for which we were woefully unprepared. All we knew was that they had begun to kill *babies*. How can they *do* that? This was *America*. As the political battle began to take shape, the lack of historical perspective among evangelicals became more and more manifest. This lack of historical understanding was harmful in two ways—and in both ways the integrity of God's Word was undermined.

---

3. In saying this, I do *not* mean that anyone who disagrees with any aspect of my thesis here is guilty of committing such a sin. I am referring to those who have believed old lies in order to promote new ones—by which I mean things like abortion rights and homosexual marriages.

The first was the result of the attempt by evangelicals to portray the pro-life movement as simply a modern form of abolitionism. We were taught that earlier Christian social "reformers" like Charles Finney were ardent abolitionists, and we pro-lifers were simply walking in his footsteps. We were taught that *Roe v. Wade* was comparable to the *Dred Scott* decision. And so we argued and talked and marched accordingly. The only problem was—it wasn't true. For the sake of a convenient argument against the monstrosity of abortion, we abandoned the clear teaching of the Bible on another subject—how slavery was to be understood and treated.

Suppose a man presented himself for membership in your church. Upon inquiring as to what he did for a living, you learned that he was an abortionist. Should he be admitted into membership? *Of course not.* Now suppose this same church was moved back in time, and a man presented himself for membership along with three of his slaves. *Now* what do you do? If he is admitted to membership, then it is clear that abortion and slavery cannot be considered to be ethically equivalent. And if he is refused membership, then what are you going to do when he (his name was Philemon) goes back and tells the apostle Paul what you did to him? For the year was not A.D. 1860 but rather A.D. 60.

It is obvious that in a fallen world, an institution like slavery will be accompanied by many attendant evils. Such evils existed with ancient Hebrew slavery, ancient Roman slavery, and with American slavery. The issue is not whether sinners will sin, but rather how Christians are *commanded* to respond to such abuses and evils. And nothing is clearer than that the New Testament opposes anything like the strident abolitionism of our country prior to the War Between the States. The New Testament contains many instructions for *Christian* slave owners, and requires a respectful submissive demeanor for Christian slaves. See, for example, "Servants, be obedient to them that are your masters according to the flesh, with fear and trembling, in singleness of your heart, as unto Christ" (Eph. 6:5–9); or "Servants, obey in all things your masters according to the flesh; not with eyeservice, as menpleasers; but in singleness of heart, fearing God" (Col. 3:22–4:1); or "And they that have believing masters, let them not despise them, because they are brethren" (I Tim. 6:1–5). At the same time, because the gospel of Christ necessarily brings liberty to captives, it should also be obvious that the spread of the gospel over time *necessarily subverts* the institution of slavery generally. But this gradual subversion would have been reformational and gradual, and not revolutionary and bloodthirsty, as radical abolitionism was.

The harm was twofold. The embarrassment of evangelicals over the plain teaching of the Bible can be put to an adept use by those currently in rebellion against God. Dr. Jerry Falwell was once in a television debate with a liberal Episcopalian bishop, and sad to say, the liberal bishop mauled Dr. Falwell. They were debating some issue like abortion or sodomy, and Falwell was maintaining the biblical position, and the bishop responded by saying, "Yes, but the Bible allows for *slavery*." Now what was Dr. Falwell going to do on national television? Does he say that the bishop is correct, the Bible does allow for slavery, and that he has no problem with it? We can see the headlines of the *New York Times* now: "Falwell Fires on Ft. Sumter." Or perhaps he could have said that the bishop was wrong—but the good bishop was right. So he did the only thing he could do in such a situation, which was to hem and haw.

On another occasion, a Christian man was handing out tracts at a gay and lesbian dance. Those attending the dance did not appear to be pleased with this, and someone apparently called a liberal Methodist pastor to come and deal with him. The minister came down, and in the course of the discussion, the Christian man said that Leviticus condemns homosexuality as an abomination. The liberal pastor responded by saying, "Yes, but the Old Testament allowed for *slavery*." The Christian responded by saying, "Yes, it certainly did. So what's your point?"

If those who hate the Word of God can succeed in getting Christians to be embarrassed by *any portion* of the Word of God, then that portion will continually be employed as a battering ram against the godly principles that are *currently* under attack. In our day, three of the principal issues are abortion, feminism, and sodomy. If we respond to the "embarrassing parts" of Scripture by saying, "That was then, this is now," we will quickly discover that unembarrassed progressives can play that game even more effectively than embarrassed conservatives can.[4] Paul prohibited eldership to women? *That was then, this is now.* Moses condemned sodomy? *That was then, this is now.*

In a certain sense, I am backing into our discussion of the War Between the States. We have been told many times that the war was over slavery, but in my view it was actually over the biblical meaning of constitutional government.[5] The *inflammatory* issue has become slavery, however, and so the real issue is obscured in the minds of many.

But is this not curious? The reason why many Christians will be tempted to dismiss the arguments presented here is that I am saying (out loud) that a godly man in 1850 could have been a slave owner. But this "inflammatory" position is the very point upon which the Bible *speaks most directly*, again and again. In other words, more people will struggle with what I am saying at the point where the Bible speaks most clearly. There is no exegetical vagueness here. Not only is the Bible *not* politically correct in modern eyes, it was not politically correct one hundred and fifty years ago.

This reality points to the need for Christians to learn the biblical way of avoiding "problem texts." This is the way of *a priori* submission. Christians must recognize that they are under the authority of God and they may not develop their ideas of what is "right" and "fair" apart from the Word of God. And when the Bible is our only standard of right and wrong, problem texts disappear. This entire

---

4. Why do we call them progressives? What are they progressing *to*? Why do we call them liberals? They aren't very liberal at all. In our recent conflicts with them, we have simply taken to calling them *intoleristas*, which seems to fit far better.

5. The war occurred because Lincoln ignored the covenantal nature of the Constitution when he decided to keep states in the Union by force. Up to this point, the right of secession was the states' final check against the nationalistic centralizing impulse typified by Alexander Hamilton, Henry Clay, and Abraham Lincoln. The great classicist Basil Gildersleeve once said that the war was fought over a point of grammar. Shall we say, "The United States *is* going to . . ." or "The United States *are* going to . . ."?

issue of slavery is a wonderful issue upon which to practice. Our humanistic and democratic culture regards slavery *in itself* as a monstrous evil, *malum in se*, and it acts as though this were self-evidently true. The Bible permits Christians in slave-owning cultures to own slaves, provided they are treated well. You are a Christian. Whom do you believe?

Of course, in posing this question, I am certainly *not* wishing for a return to slavery. I am profoundly grateful that chattel slavery no longer exists in our nation. Let there be no mistake here—the logic of the Christian gospel is contradictory to the institution of slavery *generally*, and as the gospel of salvation progresses through history, one of the necessary results is the gradual eradication of all slavery. Jesus Christ really is the ultimate Jubilee. But this is not accomplished through revolutionary means, through the bloodletting of social cataclysm. Rather, it is accomplished the way yeast transforms a loaf of bread. The change is reformational and never revolutionary. And this is why the New Testament presupposes that members of Christian churches in good standing can be *either* slaves or slaveholders, and both categories are taught that in Christ there is neither slave nor free (Gal. 3:28). What those slaves and slaveholders are commanded to do is serve God faithfully in the station where He has placed them. This command had obvious ramifications in the slaveholding society into which Christ came—but it had just as obvious ramifications for Christians in the slaveholding society of the antebellum South.

A Brief Overview

In the early nineteenth century, the intellectual leadership of the North apostatized from their previous cultural commitment to the Christian faith. In my view, the watershed event in this regard was the capture of Harvard by the Unitarians in 1805. This cultural apostasy was not nearly as advanced in the South, although there were some signs of it there as well. By the time of the war, the intellectual leadership of the South was conservative, orthodox, and Christian. In contrast, the leadership of the North was radical and

Unitarian. This is not to say there were no Christians in the North, or that no faithful believers fought for the North. It is simply the recognition that on the slavery issue the drums of war were being beaten by the abolitionists, who were in turn driven by a zealous hatred of the Word of God. There were of course other causes for the conflict apart from slavery (including pressing issues like tariffs and internal improvements)—but to the extent that slavery was an issue, the radical abolitionists were in conflict with the teaching of the New Testament.

The revival that took place in the Confederate army during the war was so widespread that it has been estimated that (with the possible exception of Cromwell's army) the Confederate Army was the largest body of evangelicals under arms in the history of the world. But this of course raises the obvious question—if the South was so "right" and "Christian" as all that, then why did she lose the war? Didn't *God* know how right the South was? We must reject the childish mentality which seeks to engage in mindless partisanship at the expense of the truth. All attempts to say that the North represented nothing good, and that the South contained nothing sinful are examples of this kind of infantilism. R. L. Dabney made the point that the South lost the war *because she was under the judgment of God.*

When northern Israel led the way in rebellion against God, the conservatism of southern Judah did not avoid final apostasy, but simply traveled that path more slowly than Israel to the north. In a similar way, the South had not been entirely free from the various currents of unbelief. J. H. Thornwell was *unsuccessful* in his attempt to get the Confederate States to acknowledge the lordship of Christ.[6] So although the Southern culture represented much that was admirable, the biblical principle remains—to whom much is given, much is required. And although the South was correct about the central constitutional and cultural issues of that war,

---

6. As Genovese summarized it, "Vague recognition of God would not do. The State must recognize the triune God of the Bible—the Father, Son, and Holy Ghost" (*The Southern Front*, 40).

southern diehards must learn the hard lesson of Habakkuk, who had to accept that God can use an ungodly nation to judge another nation which is "not as bad" (Hab. 1:13). In this view, the severe judgment that befell the South *from the hand of God* was true justice in part because of how the South had treated her slaves. So this essay should *not* be taken as minimizing in any way a sin that God judged so severely.

On a related front, some Christians balk at having a sympathetic view of the South (to any extent, at any level) because they know that racism is evil. This following point is a very important point to emphasize. Like radical abolitionism, all forms of race hatred or racial vainglory are forms of rebellion against God. Such things are to be vigorously opposed because the Word of God opposes them. In brief, God has raised up all nations from one man (Acts 17:26). We are all cousins. And not only are the races connected through God's creation of Adam, we are united (this time in harmony) in the redemption purchased by the Son of God. "You are worthy to take the scroll, and to open its seals; for You were slain, and have redeemed us to God by your blood out of every tribe and tongue and people and nation, and have made us kings and priests to our God; and we shall reign on the earth" (Rev. 5:9–10).

The leadership of the early church at Antioch contained at least one black man (Acts 13:1). And what happened to Miriam when she opposed the marriage of Moses to a black woman (Num. 12)? God turned her a little bit whiter than she had been previously, but it was the white of leprosy, and this was not generally taken as an improvement. As Christians, we regard the gift at Pentecost to be a great reversal of Babel, and we believe that our missionary efforts will eventually result in the elimination of all racial hatreds *in Christ*—the only way such hatreds *can* be eliminated.

Because of a strong popular bigotry against the South, it is necessary for me to assert as strongly as I can that racism and sympathy for the Southern cause are not necessary companions. Rather, when biblically understood, they are antithetical. In my view, the natural economic death of slavery in our nation would have been hastened had there been more widespread obedience to the Word of God on the part of everyone—radical abolitionists, slaves, and slave owners. So wherever true racism appears (North, South, East, or West), or whenever it appears (in this century or the last), it must be opposed by consistent Christians. But this opposition to racism does not require us to be ignorant of the great theological and cultural issues that were at stake in the war. This is necessary because these same foundational issues are still with us today, and all of them reduce to the practical authority of Scripture.

Sodomites parade in the streets, claiming that if we do not appropriate more money to study why people with foul sexual habits get sick, we are somehow violating their civil rights. Feminists, in rebellion against God, invert the order of the home established by God, doing so in a way that seeks to rob women of their glory in biblical marriage and their security in being loved. For over three decades, we have seen over forty million unborn children slaughtered in abortion clinics. How did we get here, and what is the way out? The question cannot be answered fully without careful study of the War Between the States and the controversies surrounding it. Slavery was one of those controversies.

The Bible's View of Slavery

The Bible is not silent on the subject of slavery. We must be careful, however, if we use the phrase *biblical slavery*. What do we mean by it? A common confusion blurs an important distinction between *Hebrew* slavery—i.e., slavery in a nation covenanted with God, with laws received from His hand—and the slavery that is seen in the pages of the New Testament. In the former, we see how God's laws govern and regulate the practice of slavery in a nation called by His name and covenanted with Him. In the latter, we see God's laws as they teach His people how to live within a culture having *ungodly* laws concerning slavery. In the Roman Empire, the system of slavery was, along with the rest of that culture, in rebellion against the true and living God. In the Hebrew republic, slavery was akin to what we would call indentured servanthood—the only permanent slaves were foreigners (Lev. 25:44–46) or Hebrews who voluntarily submitted themselves to a more permanent servile status (Exod. 21:5–6). But in the Greco-Roman world, the system of slavery was pagan from top to bottom, front to back, with the slaves having virtually no recognized rights at all. "Although we do have documentary evidence for manumissions, we encounter still more bills of sale and wills, which consider slaves not as persons but as things, as *ta somata doulika*, slave bodies."[7] So a vast difference exists between the laws God gave to His own covenant people for the regulation of slavery among themselves and the laws God gave to His covenant people to regulate their conduct in the midst of a pagan system.

When we ask the question whether slavery in the South was a biblical slavery, the answer must consequently be *yes* and *no*. Was the South a nation in covenant with the Lord Jesus Christ? Had it undertaken formally to shape all its laws, including its laws on slavery, to the laws of Scripture? The answer is clearly *no*—in this sense, the South was not a Christian nation. If, however, we ask whether the South contained many conscientious Christians, both slave-owning and enslaved, who endeavored to follow the requirements of Scripture set down in the New Testament for believers in slave-holding societies, then the answer is *yes*. Not surprisingly, the large number of these believers in the Old South did have the effect of "Christianizing" it, but the process was by no means complete.

This means that the system of slave-holding in the South was far more humane than that of ancient Rome, although it still fell short of the biblical requirements for it. Were there many unbelieving slave-owners who treated their slaves unjustly? No doubt. Nevertheless, the Scriptures teach how to go about addressing this kind of thing. The discipleship of the nations is a process. This means that the South was (along with all other nations) in transition from a state of pagan autonomy to one of full submission to the Lordship of Christ. Christian influence in the South was considerable and extensive, but the laws of the South still fell short

7. Jennifer Glancy, *Slavery in Early Christianity* (Oxford: Oxford Univ. Press, 2002), 7.

of the biblical pattern. In spite of this, the Christian influence on antebellum Southern culture surpassed most other nations in the world of that time.

Nevertheless, God's law does not grade on a curve, and Southern sanctification fell drastically short of the biblical standard at a number of points. This is why someone like R. L. Dabney could maintain the relative justice of the Southern cause, and at the same time acknowledge that the South lost the war because of her sins. "A righteous God, for our sins toward Him, has permitted us to be overthrown by our enemies and His."[8]

When we turn to individuals and families, the situation is very different. The radical abolitionists maintained that slave-owning was inherently immoral under *any* circumstance. But in this matter, the Christians who owned slaves in the South were on firm scriptural ground. May a Christian own slaves, even when this makes him a part of a larger pagan system which is not fully scriptural, or perhaps not scriptural at all? Provided he owns them in conformity to Christ's laws governing such situations, the Bible is clear that under such conditions Christians may own slaves:

> Let as many bondservants as are under the yoke count their masters *worthy of all honor,* so that the name of God and His doctrine may not be blasphemed. And those who have *believing masters,* let them not despise them because they are brethren, but rather serve them because those who are benefited are believers and beloved. Teach and exhort these things. If anyone teaches otherwise and does not consent to wholesome words, even *the words of our Lord Jesus Christ,* and to the doctrine which accords with godliness, he is proud, knowing nothing. (I Tim. 6:1–4a, emphasis mine)

The slavery of Rome was anti-scriptural, and because of the great evil of the slave trade, the larger system of slavery in the South was certainly unscriptural and evil as well. Nevertheless, the Bible prohibits us from saying that slave *owning* in such contexts is

8. Dabney, *Defense,* 356.

necessarily sin. The Bible teaches that a man may be a faithful Christian and a slave owner in a pagan slave system. If he owns slaves, then Scripture *does* put a series of requirements on him, which the Church of Christ may and must insist upon. In fact, the Church must discipline in terms of those requirements.[9] But beyond those requirements, *the church may not presume to legislate.*

> Bondservants, be obedient to those who are your masters according to the flesh, with fear and trembling, in sincerity of heart, as to Christ; doing the will of God from the heart, with goodwill doing service, as to the Lord, and not to men, knowing that whatever good anyone does, he will receive the same from the Lord, whether he is a slave or free. And you, masters, do the same things to them, giving up threatening, knowing that your own Master also is in heaven, and there is no partiality with Him. (Eph. 6:5–9)

Paul says something very similar elsewhere (Col. 3:22–4:1). As far as the apostle was concerned, nothing can be plainer than the fact that a Christian could simultaneously be a slave owner and a member in good standing in a Christian church.

I am a minister, and many of the issues become clear if the proper question is properly asked. Today if an abortionist sought membership at my church, he would be refused unless he repented and abandoned his murderous practice. But if our churches had existed in the antebellum South, and a godly slave owner who treated his slaves with kindness sought membership, I could not refuse him without seeking to be holier than Christ. Such a desire would be wicked, and this wickedness was at the heart of the radical abolitionist dogma.

Having said all this, I want to grant that a very plausible argument against slavery comes from the acknowledged wickedness of the slave trade. For example, Gary DeMar has argued that because

---

9. This is one of the places where the Christian Church in the South fell short. The fact that the civil government (for example) did not prohibit the separation of slave families did not mean that the church could not discipline slaveholding members who did such a thing. See Genovese, *A Consuming Fire*, 21.

the Bible prohibits man-stealing (Exod. 21:16; I Tim. 1:10), Christians could not consistently participate at *any* point in a process that resulted from the man-stealing. "He who kidnaps a man and sells him, or if he is found in his hand, shall surely be put to death" (Exod. 21:16).

Before discussing whether slave-owning in itself necessarily constitutes an *indirect* support of this capital offense, we should first ask if believers in the South engaged in direct opposition to the acknowledged evil of the slave trade. Here, the answer is clearly in the affirmative. R. L. Dabney, in his *Defense of Virginia and the South*, begins his chapter on the slave trade with these words: "This iniquitous traffick. . . ."[10] The duty of southern Christians was clear—they had to oppose the slave trade. It is a fact that many of them did so, fervently and zealously. Dabney's vehement attack on the slave trade was representative of many other Christians who were interested in reforming Southern laws regarding slavery.

Were they hypocrites in this opposition because they raised the cry against the slave trade while indirectly supporting that trade by owning slaves? Not at all. The *Bible* defines hypocrisy. Remember that in ancient Rome the acquisition of slaves was not according to the law of God either. A Christian slave owner in that system, like Philemon, was duty-bound to oppose those features of that society, to the extent he had anything to do with it, and at the same time was required to treat his own slaves in a gracious and thoughtful manner. He was not required to release his individual slaves because of a *general* societal disobedience. He was not even required to release his slaves if they came into the Christian faith (I Tim. 6:1–4). At the same time he needed to acknowledge that his believing slaves were now Christ's freemen, and *they* were called to take any opportunity for freedom provided for them.

> Let every man abide in the same calling wherein he was called. Art thou called being a servant? care not for it: but if thou mayest be made free, use it rather. For he that is called in the Lord, being a

10. Dabney, *Defense*, 27.

servant, is the Lord's freeman: likewise also he that is called, being free, is Christ's servant. Ye are bought with a price; be not ye
the servants of men. Brethren, let every man, wherein he is called,
therein abide with God. (I Cor. 7:20–24)

As mentioned earlier, in our nation the logic of this would have
worked its way out over time in a peaceful and *Christian* form of
emancipation, without 620,000 slain.

Secondly, we must also remember that the consequences and
ramifications of the African slave trade went far beyond the situation described in Exodus 21. In that situation, when the kidnapper
was discovered, he would be tried and executed, and the one kidnapped would be restored to his home. The issues were simple and
clear. With the slave trade, the vast majority of the slaves had already been enslaved *in Africa* by other blacks. They were then taken
down to the coast and sold to the traders. The traders transported
them, usually under extreme and wicked conditions, to those places
where a market existed for their labor, but where the civil leaders
had repeatedly *and consistently* tried to stop the slave traders. One of
those places, Virginia, had attempted on no less than twenty-eight
occasions to arrest the slave trade, but was stopped by other (non-
Virginian) authorities. If the slaves were not sold in the South, they
were taken on to Haiti and Brazil, where the condition and treatment of slaves was simply horrendous.[11] The restoration of these
slaves to their former condition was a physical impossibility. Now,
under *these* conditions, was it a sin for a Christian to purchase such
a slave, knowing that he would take him home and treat him the

11. According to Fogel and Engerman, "It is customary to date the beginning of the
New World traffic in Africans in the year 1502 when the first references to blacks appear in the documents of Spanish colonial administrators." It lasted for over 350 years,
during which time "more than 9,500,000 Africans were forcibly transported across the
Atlantic. Brazil was by far the largest single participant in the traffic, accounting for 38
percent of the total. The British- and French-owned colonies in the Caribbean and the
far-flung Spanish-American empire were the destination of 50 percent. Dutch, Danish,
and Swedish colonies took another 6 percent. The remaining 6 percent represent the
share of the United States" (*Time on the Cross: The Economics of American Negro Slavery* [New
York: Norton, 1989 (reissued 1995)], 15).

way the Bible requires? If he did not purchase him, nothing would be done to improve the slave's condition, and much could happen that would make it worse. The slaves were not stolen cars; they were human beings—and I want to argue that the many Christians who treated them lawfully were in no way disobedient. We also need to recall many of the slaves in the South were descendants of men and women who had been brought over *generations* before, complicating an already complicated picture.

The requirement for godly treatment of slaves by individual masters is clearly laid out in the Bible. The requirement for a godly prohibition of man-stealing on the part of the civil magistrate is also required in the Bible. On both counts, there were many southern Christians who distinguished themselves in carefully seeking to implement *both* requirements. Their personal treatment of slaves was kind and not cruel, and their political agitation for a godly abolition of the slave trade was equally notable. Virginia was the *first* commonwealth in the world to outlaw the practice, and this after many previous unsuccessful attempts. Dabney said it well: "Virginia has the honour of being the first Commonwealth on earth to declare against the African slave trade, and to make it a penal offense. Her action antedates by thirty years the much bepraised legislation of the British parliament, and by ten years the earliest movement of Massachusetts on the subject."[12] In 1771, Virginia appealed to the King to stop the trade, saying that they had long regarded it as a practice of "great inhumanity." In 1778, Virginia prohibited the introduction of slaves into their state. Georgia was the first state to write a prohibition of the slave trade into its constitution. And we must remember that the Confederate Constitution outlawed the slave trade.[13]

The slave trade was an abomination. The Bible condemns it, and all who believe the Bible are bound to do the same. But apart from the slave trade, in a slave-holding society owning slaves per se was *not* an abomination. The Bible does not condemn it outright, and

12. Dabney, *Defense*, 50.
13. Article I, Section 9.

those who believe the Bible are bound to refrain in the same way. But if we were to look in history for Christians who reflected this biblical balance—i.e., a hatred of the slave trade and an acceptance of slavery in itself under certain conditions—we will find ourselves looking at reform-minded Christians in the antebellum South. To conclude this point, Dabney is worth quoting again:

> It is one of the strange freaks of history, that this commonwealth, which was guiltless in this thing, and which always presented a steady protest against the enormity, should become, in spite of herself, the home of the largest number of African slaves found within any of the States, and thus, should be held up by Abolitionists as the representative of the "sin of slaveholding;" while Massachusetts, which was, next to England, the pioneer and patroness of the slave trade, and chief criminal, having gained for her share the wages of iniquity instead of the persons of the victims, has arrogated to herself the post of chief accuser of Virginia.[14]

To say the least, it is strange that the thing the Bible condemns (slave-trading) brings very little opprobrium upon the North, yet that which the Bible allows (slave-ownership) has brought down all manner of condemnation upon the South.

A Very Human Time

We live in a time when people often react to what they think you might be *about* to say, instead of dealing with what in fact you did say. Or they are appalled at where they think you must be going. If some hapless scholar decided (in all innocence) that Hitler actually killed 5.5 million Jews, he would instantly be assailed as a *defender* of the Reich, for "No one would *ever* diminish the horror of the Holocaust unless he had nefarious motives." So let me be clear about this (again). My interest in this discussion is not to show the South as a perfect place for blacks to be slaves in, but rather to show the Bible as the perfect book for Christians, then and now.

14. Dabney, *Defense*, 43.

In the several quotations that follow, the point is not to paint the South as a utopia. If the institution of slavery, as it was actually practiced in the South, had been one of horror upon horror, an apocalyptic evil, then of course the New Testament strictures on masters and slaves would not apply (because these strictures were not written for times of apocalyptic evil, but rather for normal sinners). But if the antebellum South was made up of normal sinners trying to make a profit by farming, and not by fiends running death camps from Georgia to Missouri, then the New Testament requirements do apply—straight across.

Fogel and Engerman object to the common portrayal of the slaveholders:

> Both masters and slaves are painted as degraded brutes. Masters are vile because they are the perpetrators of unbridled exploitation; slaves are vile because they are the victims of it. How true to life is the portrait?[15]

We have just emerged from a century that produced a record number of moral monsters—Stalin, Hitler, Pol Pot, Mao, Idi Amin, and more. We have seen enough of them that you would think we would know what they looked like by now. They do not look like the slaveholders of the American South. If the reader likes, he may simply note that my point can be summarized by saying that men like Robert E. Lee, Thomas Jefferson, and R. L. Dabney could never be included on the same list without slandering them. The greater part of the story of slavery in the United States is a record of ordinary, sinful men living in ordinary, sinful times. Some of those sinful men trusted in Christ, and they turned to the Bible to understand what He would have them do. We could do far worse than to imitate them in this.

---

15. Fogel and Engerman, *Time on the Cross*, 109. As their subsequent discussion shows (109–144), the answer to the question is "not very."

The Problems of Slavery

Nevertheless, slavery *was* attended with many evils. As it existed in the South, it was not in any way idyllic. As a social institution, generally considered, it *was* an evil. As discussed earlier, Christians should be quick to notice the discrepancies between the biblical standards for slavery and the way slavery was practiced in the South. These differences between the biblical standard and Southern slavery make it impossible to offer an unqualified defense of the institution as it existed and operated in the South. As mentioned earlier, that institution, as it was established and defended, *invited and received the judgment of God.* Eugene Genovese, a modern and sympathetic critic of the South, rightly named this judgment "a consuming fire."[16]

Furthermore, on an individual level, the cruel mistreatment given to some slaves is inexcusable and truly despicable. All such evil was wicked and indefensible. When modern Christians condemn such things, however, they must recognize that they are *not* condemning something defended by godly Christians in the South. All such mistreatment was reprobated by the majority of antebellum Southerners as well. Modern condemnations of these abuses are several centuries late.

Finally, slavery gave an issue to radical revolutionaries through which they could provoke animosity against the South and, consequently, against the "old order" which held sway in this nation prior to 1861. The war that resulted gave these radicals an opportunity to increase the size and power of the federal government in this nation to previously undreamed-of proportions. Our nation, after 1865, was transformed into a distinctly different entity than it had been before. The nation established by the founding fathers—a limited, constitutional republic, a union of free States—was no more. And the modern, messianic State which seeks to bring us salvation by politics and law was firmly established.

---

16. Genovese, *A Consuming Fire*, 125–127. To my knowledge, this is simply the best book available on the relationship of slavery and the evangelical Christians in the South.

Conclusion

None need lament the passing of slavery, and I most emphatically do not lament it. But Genovese provides the needed balance:

> Let us thank God for slavery's demise. But however badly the pro-slavery social theorists, clerical and lay, erred in their proposed solution to the great social question of their—and our—day, they offered a profound analysis of the relation between social order and the prospects for upholding sound Christian doctrine.[17]

Who cannot lament the damage to both white and black that has occurred as a consequence of the *way* in which slavery was abolished? I am forced to say that, in many ways, the remedy which has been applied has resulted in problems that are every bit as bad as the original disease ever was. Christians who doubt this should consider whether it was safer to be a black child in the womb in 1858 or in 2005.

The issue of slavery was used to provoke a revolution in 1861. That revolution has continued to this day with ongoing and very destructive results. It is time for us to stand and declare the truth about slavery and to expose the failures of the abolitionist world-view. Having done this, we must go on to proclaim the only truth which can set all men truly free from every form of slavery—the gospel of our Lord Jesus Christ.

17. Ibid., 121.

5.

Plowing the Same Ground

My intent in this presentation is twofold. First, I would like to demonstrate what our stated point was in publishing *Southern Slavery as It Was* in 1996.[1] Not wanting to invent new (and more defensible) reasons *after* we were called on the carpet, I would like to show more clearly what we really did say at that time. Rather than engage in revisionist explanations for our conduct, I would like to reconstruct our basic argument from quotations taken from that booklet. I would then like to assemble the points made into a general argument. Having done so, I would like to go over some of the same ground again in order to present further arguments and documentation.

In a section entitled "So Why Are We Writing About *This?*" we pointed out that in 1973, "the Supreme Court had ruled that it was unconstitutional for the various states to outlaw the dismemberment of the unborn."[2] This alarmed Christians greatly, as it ought to have done. But evangelical Christians are not renowned for their historical sense, and so they responded to this attack on human dignity in two ways. It was our contention that both these initial responses (however well-intentioned) undermined what evangelicals were actually trying to accomplish in resisting the new abortion culture, and that in order to resist the abortion culture root and

1. Wilkins and Wilson, *Southern Slavery as It Was*.
2. Ibid., 9.

branch, a different understanding of certain things (like slavery) was necessary.

To revisit the point briefly, the first harmful evangelical response was to try to equate pro-life and abolitionism. This response was understandable on the surface because the Supreme Court was involved in both the *Dred Scott* case and *Roe v. Wade.* The difficulty was that in order to defend the Bible's teaching on abortion, we had to abandon its teaching on slavery. And if we did *our* picking and choosing, what would prevent our adversaries from doing the same? Suppose they said, "Why don't *we* accept what the Bible teaches on slavery and reject what it teaches on abortion? Special thanks to the evangelicals for showing us the way!" Using the Bible as a grab bag from which to pick and choose the texts we find acceptable is hardly a scriptural worldview.

The second harmful response was a direct result of the first. When we set aside the teaching of Scripture on slavery, and began to equivocate on what the Bible actually teaches, it was soon discovered that nonbelievers would not let us get away with it. It turns out that there are actual non-Christians out there who have read the Bible and who know what it says. This led to Christians being convicted, and rightly so, of special pleading when it came our defense of the unborn. Should we let the fetus live because Moses came down from the mount and told us not to kill? If we say *yes,* then the astute nonbeliever would almost immediately point out that Moses taught some *other* things as well.

So the argument we presented in our booklet ran this way. Evangelicals were rightly outraged at the inhumanity being mandated by the secularists who had somehow (mysteriously!) gotten control of the courts. But because they were unaware of the intellectual history behind the Supreme Court decision, evangelicals tried to see themselves as carrying on the abolitionist tradition, when that abolitionist tradition actually embodied the very radicalism that they were engaged in fighting. This meant, in its turn, that conservative Christians could easily be charged with inconsistency when it came to applying the teaching of Scripture.

There were some other issues swirling behind the scenes around this time as well. There were some pro-lifers who actually *did* embody the radicalism of the abolitionists. For one example, Paul Hill murdered an abortion doctor in Florida in the summer of 1994, two years before our publication of the booklet. He has since been executed for that murder by the state of Florida. Prior to this time, Paul Hill had been a member of a conservative Presbyterian church in Florida (the pastor of which is a good friend of mine). He was excommunicated by that church for his radicalism *before* the murder. Hill saw himself (accurately enough) in the tradition of John Brown, and the faithful church that rejected him saw themselves as faithful theological heirs of Southern conservatives. Paul Hill had attended Reformed Theological Seminary at the same time Steve Wilkins was studying there, and before the murder of the abortionist, Wilkins spent many hours with Hill on the phone trying to dissuade him from his growing radicalism.

In 1996, *Credenda/Agenda* magazine, which I edit, published the editorial "Moving Beyond Pro-Life" that represented a definitive break with the radical "abolitionism" that had infected certain quarters of the pro-life movement. This was the same year the *Southern Slavery* booklet was published. Paul Hill, by then in prison, wrote the magazine a response, which is still on the official Paul Hill website.

Being a little bit radical is like being a little bit pregnant. We were interested in developing a full-orbed biblical response to the secularist jihad against the Christian faith, and we were not interested in resisting the onslaught by simply retreating to an earlier form of approved compromise. We therefore argued that the only Christian response to our current culture wars that God would honor and bless is a response that refused to apologize for *anything* in the Bible: "Christians must recognize that they are under the authority of God, and they may not develop their ideas of what is 'right' and 'fair' apart from the Word of God."[3]

3. Ibid., 12.

We argued that a thoroughgoing Christian response to our current culture wars (abortion, radical feminism, sodomite marriage) had to be based on an unapologetic acceptance of the absolute authority of Scripture over *everything*: "If those who hate the Word of God can succeed in getting Christians to be embarrassed by *any portion* of the Word of God, then that portion will continually be employed as a battering ram against the godly principles that are *currently* under attack."[4]

We held that the scriptural teaching on slavery (Old Testament and New) had obvious relevance for all slave-owning societies, including the antebellum South. "But this 'inflammatory' position is the very point upon which the Bible speaks most clearly, again and again."[5] "The Bible is not silent on the subject of slavery."[6]

We urged Christians to consider the damage caused by our national disobedience in that war. Had we addressed the sinfulness of the system of slavery in the way that God required (reformation, not revolution), 620,000 men would not have died, and our country would not have seen the massive governmental centralization that came about as a result of that conflict. You cannot have the hatred generated in such a war disappear overnight either: "None need lament the passing of slavery. But who cannot but lament the damage to both white and black that has occurred as a consequence of the *way* it was abolished? . . . The issue of slavery was used to provoke a revolution in 1861. That revolution has continued to this day."[7] The point here was that the revolution that made it possible for the federal government to impose an atrocity like *Roe v. Wade* on the several states was a revolution that began in earnest in 1861.

The section of the booklet that characterized the institution of slavery in the South as comparatively benign served a related purpose. The point was not to laud American slavery as a positive good, but rather to show that it was benign when compared with

4. Ibid., 11.
5. Ibid., 11–12.
6. Ibid., 15.
7. Ibid., 39.

ancient Roman slavery (concerning which St. Paul wrote), the slavery that existed elsewhere in the Western Hemisphere (Haiti and Brazil), and the rhetoric of the abolitionists. We sought to describe slavery "as it was" in order to show that Scripture applied to the situation. That we were not interested in defending the abuses of slavery as they occurred on the ground in our country can be illustrated by a response I wrote to one critic:

> Please remember that throughout our booklet, in describing features of Southern slavery, we used words like *deplorable, wicked, evil, despicable, cruel, inexcusable, abuse, immorality,* and, following Dabney, *criminal barbarity.* Now here is a simple Golden Rule question. Would anyone who had *not* read our booklet, but who had read McKenzie's article about it, gotten *this* impression of what we really believe (and plainly said) about such things? The answer is *no.* So why should I believe that McKenzie has special competence in representing Southerners who have been dead for more than a century, *when I know for a fact* that he has grossly misrepresented *this* Southerner, despite the fact that I went out of my way to condemn in round numbers every Southern sin I could think of?[8]

The reason for placing the sins of the South in this kind of context is straightforward. The southern treatment of their slaves (as it generally was) shows that the situation was the kind of situation which required that the teaching of the New Testament be followed because it was preeminently applicable to that situation. If St. Paul returned Onesimus to Philemon (and he did), what would he have us do when a similar scenario played out in Virginia in 1856?

So then, here is our argument, presented as though it were a juice concentrate:

---

8. From my response to a privately circulated paper (now public), "Doug Wilson and Steve Wilkins on Slavery and the Civil War" by Dr. Tracy McKenzie, submitted to the elders of Eastside Evangelical Fellowship, Bellevue, Washington. See "Fragments from the Controversy" elsewhere in this volume, especially pages 101–102, where the excerpted passage is in context.

Christians must live or die by the Scriptures, as they stand. Compromise on what the Bible teaches about slavery is directly related to the current pressures to compromise on abortion and sodomy. Southern slavery was an example of the kind of sinful human situation that called for diligent obedience to St. Paul's directives, on the part of both masters and slaves. Because this did not happen, and because of the way slavery ended, the federal government acquired the power to impose things on the states that it did not have before. Therefore, for all these reasons, radicalism is to be rejected by Christians.

Having said all this, and being able to point to places in the booklet where we in fact said all this, let me nevertheless grant that some still did not grasp the point we were making. This is attributable, no doubt, to a number of factors. The booklet was only thirty-nine pages long, and we were addressing a subject (the War Between the States) that according to one author has generated around 50,000 books. "More has been written on the subject than almost any other event in human history."[9] It is difficult to anticipate every objection. The war is a subject on which feelings still run high. Steve Wilkins and I were and are imperfect communicators. Some of our readers were imperfect readers, and a few of them were overtly hostile and dishonest readers. At any rate, however it happened, let me simply assert now that this is in fact the argument. This is the issue, the point behind publishing *Southern Slavery as It Was*, a point that I still find impossible to back away from or apologize for.

In that vein, let me take a little extra space to reinforce some of the points made. One of the complaints made about our booklet was that certain things were simply asserted or assumed that needed to be documented. But as I appeal to other authorities, allow me to note that I don't think this will really satisfy a certain kind of critic. This subject is like a tightly knit sweater. Find a little Irish pennant on the right arm, pull on it long enough, and the left arm will begin to unravel. One thing will always lead to another, and answering one objection will simply generate another objection.

9. Jeffrey Hummel, *Emancipating Slaves, Enslaving Free Men* (Chicago: Open Court, 1996), 3.

In response to one critic, I wrote that there really was a Southern intellectual conservative tradition, and that I was in it. I expressed my indebtedness to Richard Weaver, author of *Ideas Have Consequences* and *The Southern Tradition at Bay*. The critic's response to this was simply to dismiss Weaver as an "English professor." Clearly not a trained historian. So let me begin my quotations by citing one of America's foremost historians on the subject of slavery and the War Between the States, Eugene Genovese, on the subject of . . . Richard Weaver.

> As the intellectual leader of the southern conservative movement, Bradford assumed the mantle of his great predecessor, Richard Weaver, the formidable post-World War II social critic whose work, also, remains unread in Academia. Weaver's *The Southern Tradition at Bay* and *The Southern Essays of Richard Weaver* constitute a searing critique of the principal ideological tendencies in Western civilization and as fine a history of postbellum southern thought as we have.[10]

The controversies surrounding this subject are another example of what I have elsewhere called "paradigm bumper cars." I do not believe any citations of this nature will convince the inconvincible. But there may be a few readers who are willing to consider these things, and weigh charitably the possibility that I did not manufacture all these opinions *ex nihilo*.

The person weighing these things must know that there is no publication called *All Reputable Historians' Review*. Acceptance of what one certified historian states entails rejection of what another certified historian says. This is not the path to relativism, but is rather an acceptance of what the Christian faith plainly teaches us. Men are sinners, *and this includes the historians*. A Christian study of history must include the realization that men have a universal propensity to justify themselves. This recognition should issue no waivers, meaning that the historians themselves are included in it. Not only

10. Genovese, *The Southern Front*, 258.

so, but we should be particularly skeptical of history *as written by the victors*. Historian David Donald once noted that the historian is a "camp follower of the successful army."[11] And Lord Acton said that the "historian should be a hanging judge, for the muse of history is not Clio but Rhadamanthus, the avenger of innocent blood."[12]

That said, did the outcome of the War Between the States make *Roe v. Wade* a possibility? Without a doubt. Speaking of the Fourteenth Amendment to the Constitution, Jeffrey Hummel writes this: "No other constitutional innovation has proved more momentous. It extended from the national to the state governments nearly all the restrictions on government power contained in the Bill of Rights. Thus at a single stroke it subjected much state legislation to federal review."[13] This is precisely what happened in *Roe v. Wade*. An overweening and arrogant federal government mandated the deaths of millions of Americans, and the states did not believe themselves to be in a position to resist the decree. Could this legal atrocity have happened (*judicially* speaking) in 1840?

Did the Christian apologists for slavery in the antebellum South have the advantage over the abolitionists when it came to their debates on the subject of slavery? Again, there is no question:

> The God-fearing southern people turned to the Bible to justify slavery, and the Bible did not disappoint them. Their theologians rent the abolitionists, at least on the essentials, in their war of biblical exegesis. Increasingly, the abolitionists had to retreat to arguments from the Spirit rather than the Word—a procedure that served them well among many northerners for whom the Word was becoming something of a nuisance.[14]

And again,

> Thornwell and his fellow southern divines argued—and, I regret to say, demonstrated—that the Old Testament established slavery

11. Quoted in Hummel, *Emancipating Slaves*, 351.
12. Ibid., 349.
13. Ibid., 301.
14. Genovese, *The Southern Front*, 34–35.

as ordained of God and that Jesus, who spoke not one word against it and did not exclude slaveholders from the church, reaffirmed the sanction.[15]

There are of course many other issues. Was slavery to be a permanent institution, or was it an institution bound to fall as the work of the gospel made its way through the nations? I hold the latter, and believe that the genius of the gospel brings liberty with it. But it does not do this in one fell swoop. The kingdom of God is like leaven that works its way through the loaf. The point is not whether slavery can be abused (it can be, and most certainly was). The point is not whether it must be considered a permanent fixture of human life (which I would deny). The issue is whether a Christian man could have lawfully owned a slave in 1850 America without being *necessarily* guilty of a moral outrage. Was slave ownership *malum in se*, an evil in itself? The answer to that question, for anyone who believes the Bible, is that it was possible for a godly man to own slaves, provided he treated them exactly as the Scripture required. In a sinful world, slave ownership *generally* is sinful, and it is a system that invites abuse. Over time the gospel *will* overthrow all forms of slavery. But again, the kingdom arrives like yeast working through the loaf, and not like a *coup de main*. In the meantime, to have the likes of the abolitionist Charles G. Finney (who said that it is impossible to be on the right side of God and the wrong side of the slavery issue) hurling his taunts at Abraham and Philemon is a bit thick.

Does appreciation of the South's cause, to any extent, require us to lose all moral perspective, and embrace sectionalism over scriptural principle? No—just the reverse. We do not gloss over the sins of the South. We do not defend them. We have no responsibility with regard to them other than simple repentance. But that repentance means that we must look toward Christ, always and only, through the Spirit and the Word *together.* "Despite sins which are as scarlet, the South has remained a Christian country in that it

15. Ibid., 37.

has persisted in describing the relationship of man to the universe in religious symbols."[16] Flannery O'Connor once pointed to this kind of inadequate residue as describing a Christ-haunted South. For those of us who are seeking a recovery of the Reformed faith in its fullness, this is obviously not enough, and has to be seen as a ministry of the law rather than of grace. But the law is a schoolmaster to bring us to Christ.

16. Richard Weaver, *The Southern Tradition at Bay: A History of Postbellum Thought* (Washington, D.C.: Regnery Gateway, 1989), 27.

6.

Black Confederates

FOR THE RELATIVIST, obviously, no absolute truth can exist any-where. Consistency in this view is hard to come by; it always needs working up to gradually, and even then it falls short. A relativistic rebellion can never occur all at once, but rather begins where the sinful heart of man chafes most quickly under the government of absolutes—sexual ethics, dogmatic theology, and so on. At the beginning, relativists like to pretend that when "this one point" is challenged, the rest of the universe will not fly off in all directions. So after the first stages of the coup, any standing residuum of the old moral order is not taken as remaining evidence of absolute truth, but rather just plain furniture for which no account need be given. Thus it is assumed two and two will continue to equal four even though no absolute law can ever constrain one's lusts.

But ideas have destinations along with their consequences. Rela-tivism is a leaven that cannot be limited to immoral sexual activ-ity or a rejection of the creeds. Eventually *any* claim to objective truth, whether in arithmetic or science or history, must be rejected also. No truth claim may be accepted other than the one which rejects truth claims. Our current obsession with multiculturalism is a prime example of this. This obsession is not an educated desire to "modify the emphasis," gently reminding us that the Chinese had a great civilization while our Anglo ancestors were still kill-ing their meat with rocks. If the desire of the multiculturalists were simply a well-taken insistence that white people are not the only people in history who ever did anything, there would be no argument. But modern "multiculturalism" is *relativistic* and thus is not an attack on "white history." It is an attack on the very idea of objective history itself.

As a result, multiculturalism delivers a twofold insult to American blacks. In the first place they are saddled with a mandatory pride in bogus realities. Advocacy history in its "Afrocentrist" guise says that blacks taught Socrates everything he knew, blacks built the pyramids, and so forth. Intelligent blacks are embarrassed by the whole farce. "Kwandi Kweebe invented the light bulb? Oh, great. *Now* I feel empowered." The second insult, worse because it has been far more successful as a slander, consists of withholding from blacks an important part of their genuine heritage, one in which they can and should take deep satisfaction and pride.

The Confederate States of America lasted as long as it did, against overwhelming odds, in part because of the great contribution made by many loyal Confederate blacks to her war effort. This contribution is probably one of the greatest untold stories in the annals of our nation's history. Not only was it a "finest hour," to use Churchill's phrase, it was an hour which white America generally refuses to acknowledge—to this day. This was a valiant contribution *not* calculated to earn the praise of men. But even though it was not offered by men-pleasers, our duty of acknowledging this long-ignored heroism remains.

Before discussing some of the particulars, a reply should first be made to an anticipated objection. The modern egalitarian mindset is incapable of recognizing an aristocratic and feudal society, which the antebellum South was, without assuming as axiomatic that the subordinate classes must, of necessity, have been constantly seething with resentment and discontent. Therefore any black "contribution" to the cause of the South (if you can prove it, which you can't because we're not listening) must have been coerced at the end of the lash, and there ends the discussion. In the South there *was* resentment and discontent, and injustice *was* done to the blacks, but there was also a great deal more than this.

Biblical students of history know that conflicts such as the Southern War of Independence are never as tidy as the mind of the historical propagandist would like to make them. Thousands of white Southerners fought for the North. Thousands of white Northerners, called "Copperheads," were Southern sympathizers. Some states, like Maryland and Virginia, split in two. Many blacks headed north to their longed-for freedom. The Vice-President of the Federals was a native of Tennessee, and the Vice-President of the Confederacy was an ardent opponent of secession. But the king of all such oddities is the great untold oddity—the ardent support of the Confederacy by thousands of blacks, both free and slave. I want to make this point but I also want to keep it in perspective. At the end of the war, the black population was around four million. The number of blacks who fought for the South was a small handful out of this number, comparatively. But their contribution was real nonetheless, and even though it was comparatively small, no place can be made for it in modern accounts of that war. Why is this? It shouldn't take up that much space.

This black support was like the rest of the country—torn and mixed. Some blacks were trying to prove themselves. Some wanted adventure, while others were fighting for self-preservation. Many of the free blacks in the South were well-to-do slave owners themselves and they knew a Northern victory would ruin them, which it did. But the majority of blacks who supported the cause did so in order to protect the way of life they had always known.

Black Southerners were Southerners. Many of them were patriots. They were natives of a land at war, and their response to the invasion of their country should not be at all surprising. The wave of patriotic fervor which swept the South clearly included the black population. Across the South, blacks frequently and publicly offered their whole-hearted service to the cause of the Confederacy. Charles Tinsley, spokesman for Peterburg's free blacks, was representative of this: "We are willing to aid Virginia's cause to the utmost extent of our ability."[1]

Of course the central issue is not how blacks felt about the war when it first began, because emotions always run high for everyone at such a time. What did Southern blacks do to contribute tangibly to the war effort "across five Aprils"? Three areas are worthy of mention. The first is that the infrastructure of the Southern war effort was heavily dependent upon faithful and loyal black labor. The South was thoroughly dependent upon its black population, and could not do *anything*, much less go to war, without black involvement and support. Speaking of slaves, Benjamin Quarles notes the obvious—that slaves were used in the Southern war effort: "Not far behind the lines, and frequently within them, were the military laborers who threw up the foundations for the artillery, built the forts and dug the entrenchments."[2] What is not so obvious, especially to modern eyes, is the fact that, under such conditions, such work could not have been accomplished without a significant loyalty and willingness to serve. On the home front, blacks manned the mines, the munitions factories, and kept the crops growing which in turn kept the army in the field. Many black slaves stepped into the vacated role of white overseers and served there diligently.

Second, we must remember the numerous body servants who accompanied their masters to war, and who faithfully served them throughout the conflict. Regarding this, Charles Harper stated,

> No class of servants had such excellent opportunities to desert or to evidence disloyalty. Yet this class almost never deserted. Black Confederates followed their masters to war, worked as teamsters, laborers, foragers and cooks in the Confederate army, and did yeoman service, shouldering arms and burning gunpowder in combat, and when captured entered Yankee prisons as prisoners of war.[3]

1. Quoted in Ervin Jordan, Jr., *Black Confederates and Afro-Yankees in Civil War Virginia* (Charlottesville & London: Univ. Press of Virginia, 1995), 216.

2. Benjamin Quarles, *The Negro in the Civil War* (New York: Da Capo Press, 1953), xiii.

3. Quoted in Charles Kelly Barrow, J. H. Segars, and R. B. Rosenburg, eds., *Forgotten Confederates: An Anthology about Black Southerners* (Atlanta: Southern Heritage Press, 1995), 17.

This class of Confederates exhibited great courage, resourceful-ness, and loyalty. Nathan Bedford Forrest said of the servants who went to war with him that no better Confederates ever lived.

The third area, and the most controversial, is the direct contri-bution of blacks in combat. The well-known black abolitionist, Frederick Douglass, said this: "There are at the present moment, many colored men in the Confederate Army doing duty not only as cooks, servants, and laborers, but as real soldiers, having muskets on their shoulders and bullets in their pockets, ready to shoot down loyal troops and do all that soldiers may do to destroy the Federal government and build up that of the traitors and rebels."[4]

One estimate places the number of black Confederate combat-ants at around 40,000. As noted above, this is a very small number comparatively—only about one percent of the black population. At the same time it is not insignificant. The first Union officer to lose his life in combat, Major Winthrop, was probably shot by a black man.[5]

In 1862, Captain Isaac Heysinger observed the following con-cerning the Army of North Virginia:

> At 4 o'clock this morning the Rebel army began to move from our town, Jackson's force taking the advance. The movement continued until 8 o'clock P.M., occupying 16 hours. The most liberal calcu-lation could not give them more than 64,000 men. Over 3,000 Negroes must be included in the number. . . . They had arms, rifles, muskets, sabers, bowie-knives, dirks, etc. They were supplied, in many instances, with knapsacks, haversacks, canteens, etc., and they were manifestly an integral portion of the Southern Confed-eracy army. They were seen riding on horses and mules, driving wagons, riding on caissons, in ambulances, with the staff of gener-als and promiscuously mixed up with all the Rebel horde.[6]

4. Quoted in ibid., 10.
5. Ibid., 19.
6. Ibid., 22.

One Union soldier wrote a letter to the *Indianapolis Star* which was reprinted by the *New York Tribune*. It said, in part, "A body of seven hundred Negro infantry opened fire on our men, wounding two lieutenants and two privates. . . . We have heard of a regiment of Negroes at Manassas, and another at Memphis, and still another at New Orleans, but did not believe it until it came so near home and attacked our men."[7] It is important to note that rumor and panic can cause many strange stories to circulate in wartime, but it also seems apparent that blacks were involved in the Confederate war effort to some *observable* degree.

Now it is true the Confederate *national* government did not approve the use of blacks under arms until late in the war, when the cause was desperate, but the decentralized nature of the CSA must also be recognized. Many opportunities for black service existed in local and state units, and those opportunities were taken.

Blacks also served effectively as snipers. One remarkable sharpshooter would settle in tall trees, and begin to systematically pick off Union soldiers. Because of this a detachment of soldiers was sent to get him, and after much maneuvering, finally surrounded him. One of the Yanks yelled up at him, "I say big nigger, you better come down from there, you are captured." The black Confederate's last words were, "Not as this chile knows of!" He resumed fire and was immediately killed.[8]

We must recognize the *nature* of the racism that has afflicted many in the South since the war is partially the fruit of the Reconstruction and not necessarily the direct result of slavery and the war. Those southern whites who today despise blacks, far from showing ongoing resistance, are continuing to submit to that humanist nightmare which was first imposed at Reconstruction. Far better would be the attitude of Southern whites who fought and bled alongside Southern blacks. At a reunion of the 7th Tennessee Cavalry in 1876, Col. William Sanford said, "And to you our colored friends . . . we

---

7. Quoted in Richard Rollins, ed., *Black Southerners in Gray: Essays on Afro-Americans in Confederate Armies* (Murfreesboro: Southern Heritage Press, 1994), 20–21.
8. Ibid., 19–20.

say welcome. We can never forget your faithfulness in the darkest hours of our lives. We tender to you our hearty respect and love, for you never faltered in duty nor betrayed our trust."[9] There is an element in the Confederate heritage (at its best) that includes deep affection between white and black. This is not a denial that there was also great sin, and sin that included racial animosity. One wit once distinguished the racism of the North and the racism of the South in this way: in the North, people did not care how far blacks advanced, just so long as they did not get close; in the South, people did not care how close blacks got, just so long as they did not advance. Reconstruction imposed draconian terms in this regard, and the Southern paternalism turned to animosity. And of course Christians must reject every form of racial animosity or vainglory.

Nevertheless, even with all this acknowledged, some may question the wisdom of emphasizing such an issue: "We have enough problems in our culture without resurrecting a war that ended one hundred and forty years ago." This may seem as fruitful to them as a partisan rehash of the Second Punic War. But I am convinced that we will not understand the current civil conflicts which surround us until we go back and learn the truth about the War Between the States. Until we get that particular history lesson straight, we will continue to get every other subsequent history lesson wrong. The battles we fight today are simply a later stage in the same war.

The war was over the meaning of constitutional government, the nature of federalism, the life of republics, and the definition of civic liberty. Not one of these issues has become a museum piece since the close of the war, and all of them began long before the war. We cannot hope to fight the good fight now while repudiating those who fought the same fight earlier.

But still the apparently reasonable advice is offered to us: "Give it up. Let it go. Stop fighting old battles. Quit tilting at windmills. Just accept the past. Let's just do what we can now. Don't inflame old wounds. Just let it go."

Not as this chile knows of.

9. Barrow, Segars, and Rosenburg, *Forgotten Confederates*, 66.

7.

Dabney in Full

This is a lightly edited version of a talk given at our annual 2004 history confer-ence. The conference was on revolution (Robespierre, Marx, van Prinsterer), but the word had been spread by our adversaries that the conference was on slavery, and there was a general hubbub in our community in line with that misinformation. The conference was held on the grounds of the University of Idaho, which spent about $16,000 to counter the effects of our conference (and offered one academic credit for protesting us), and then charged us an extra $1000 for the security they had to provide because of all the commotion. The talk contains a few topical references to the protesters outside, and to the local situation, but I am afraid that these references do not do the situation justice.

First Introduction

Most of you know about the controversy surrounding this conference, and that more than a little of it concerns the Confederate battle flag. This is why I need to begin this talk with a little
apology: all this time, I had been under the impression that the
Confederate battle flag was simply the concert tour logo for Lynyrd
Skynyrd. But, as it turns out, there are layers of meaning here about
which I was blissfully unaware. So, it must be assumed that this
entire controversy has been most unnecessary, and so I would like
to apologize for any inconvenience that this may have caused.

I can tell that I am not fooling anyone. So let me move on to
another observation. Before speaking to our attendees, please allow

a brief digression. For the protesters outside, and any observers in Atlanta or elsewhere, I have some bad news, good news, and then some bad news again. Sorry to end on a sad note, but this is just the way it has fallen out.

The bad news for you all is that I am *not* a neo-Confederate. Despite the best efforts of lots and lots of people, the truth remains, whole and entire. I am not a neo-Confederate. Have I mentioned recently that neither my wife nor I are neo-Confederates?

But lest I leave the protesters outside disconsolate, there is good news for them, news that might possibly justify all that blind zeal. If you insist on using a phrase with *Confederate* in it, it *could* be fair to say that I am a *paleo*-Confederate—so long as you also called me a paleo-conservative, a paleo-Constantinian, a paleo-medievalist, and a paleo-Calvinist. I say this even while knowing that there are aspects of all these paleo-*non*-utopias that were every bit as atrocious as certain elements in the antebellum South. Nevertheless, as far as American history is concerned, I have certain definite views about the development and deterioration of the Christian faith on these shores, the history of the U.S. Constitution, and how all that relates to the peculiar challenges we as American Christians confront today. So if you wanted to summarize those particular American views, go ahead, use the tag *paleo-Confederate*.

But this brings us to the bad news again, at least for our protesters. In order to find out what *paleo-Confederate* means, you might have to read a book or something. I suggest beginning with *Christianity and Culture* by T. S. Eliot. But before checking it out, you do have to be assured of one thing—checking it out is most necessary. All the natural conclusions to which moderns are tempted to leap on such matters are almost entirely wrong. We are talking about things concerning which modern education has left you woefully unprepared—and it shows. For example, someone should have known that the white hands of Saruman were not a good symbol of tolerance for that display outside.

As I have waded, machete in hand, through the verbiage that this controversy has produced, I have been struck by how little *thought*

has gone into the growth of this lush and very green jungle. As I
have read editorials, letters to the editor, and heard outrageous
statements made by people who actually have drivers' licenses,
one of the things that came to mind, most naturally, was H. L.
Mencken's description of the speeches of Warren Harding. Here is
Mencken, at his inspired best:

> It reminds me of a string of wet sponges; it reminds me of tattered
> washing on the line; it reminds me of stale bean soup, of college
> yells, of dogs barking idiotically through endless nights. It is so
> bad that a sort of grandeur creeps into it. It drags itself out of a
> dark abysm . . . of pish, and crawls insanely up the topmost pin-
> nacle of posh. It is rumble and bumble. It is flap and doodle. It is
> balder and dash.[1]

In applying this kind of description to the vaporings of our
adversaries, the point is not to elicit a gut chuckle at someone else's
expense for mere entertainment purposes. The point is to identify
the desperate spiritual problem we are confronting, to call it by
its biblical name, and to call for repentance. Jesus speaks of those
who are in the grip of a self-important self-righteousness, which is
the chief characteristic of our Intoleristas, and He says that their
fundamental problem is *that they are spiritually dull.*

> For this people's heart is waxed gross, and their ears are dull of
> hearing, and their eyes they have closed; lest at any time they
> should see with their eyes, and hear with their ears, and should
> understand with their heart, and should be converted, and I should
> heal them. (Mt. 13:15)

Dullness of ear, when it comes to the words of God, inexorably
leads to dullness of everything else. And so this is why we are
confronting a culture of tedious and interminable dullness, characterized by short attention spans, sound-byte argumentation, tepid

---

1. Mencken, *On Politics: A Carnival of Buncombe* (Baltimore: Johns Hopkins, 1956),
42.

poetry, obnoxious art and architecture, techno-chattering music, unloved and therefore ugly women, unloved and rejected children, not to mention unloved and therefore dismembered children, and a culture rapidly becoming as grotesque as a Super Bowl half-time. Then we see all these placards calling for someone in the government to come and fix all our problems. But this is something the government cannot do, for the government is no Savior. Only Jesus Christ is the Savior of the world.

In this controversy, we have been hearing, *ad nauseam*, that we have a political agenda. This also is a product of dull thinking, and I trust that this talk on Dabney will help clarify what is actually occurring here. We have no political agenda, but we most certainly have an agenda for politics.

Second Introduction

As many of you know, this conference has attracted a lot of outside notice, much of it from people who have that special knack of getting things wrong. Because the theme of this conference was widely misreported far and wide, I have resolved to get through this lecture on Dabney without using the word *slavery* once. Actually, upon reflection, maybe I should make that "twice." This reminds me of the time a woman sat next to the famously taciturn President Coolidge, and bubbled happily that she had bet someone that she could get more than two words out of him that evening. "You lose," he said.

Overview of Dabney's Life

Robert Lewis Dabney was born in Virginia on the fifth of March, 1820. He died in 1898, and in between those two dates he lived one of the most remarkable lives ever to grace this nation. He was the sixth of eight children, and after his father died in 1833, as he was able, Dabney assumed the role of caring for his mother, which he did for the rest of her life.[2] He went to Hampden-Sidney College

2. A good source for the details of Dabney's life is Thomas Cary Johnson, *The Life and Letters of Robert Lewis Dabney* (Carlisle: Banner of Truth, 1977). I have used it here for this general chronology as well as for some anecdotes, which I cite separately below.

when he was sixteen, for about a year and half. It was there that he was converted in the course of a small revival at the college.

He left before graduating in order to help his mother with their farm, and after two years of this farming, he went to the University of Virginia in 1839. By 1842, he received his M.A. at the age of twenty-two. After graduating he returned to help his mother on the farm for another two years. At this point, he went to Union Theological Seminary and was licensed to preach in 1846. He served as a home missionary for a year and then received a call to the pastorate of Tinkling Springs Presbyterian Church. Here he met his wife, Margaret Lavinia Morrison, and they married in 1848. He continued to farm as well as pastor. After seven years in the pastorate here, he was called to teach at Union Theological Seminary—where he remained for the next thirty years (allowing for the disruptions in the war).

His life was remarkably successful and remarkably *hard*. Three of his six boys died of diphtheria (a fact that ought to be considered by some modern Christians who too glibly reject the blessings of immunization). Shortly before the war, in 1860, he received several prestigious offers from the North, including a professorship at Princeton, which he turned down. He could see that trouble was imminent, and he did not want to head north in such circumstances. He sold his farm at the beginning of the war for four thousand dollars and loaned the money to the Confederacy. It was, of course, never repaid. In today's money, that would be about a quarter of a million dollars. It is worth noting that this was money that he had earned himself and not money that had come to him through any inheritance.

Near the end of his life, about ten years before he died, he went completely blind. In all this, we can see that his life was marked by the successes that attended his remarkable gifts, which were generally acknowledged everywhere he went, but also by numerous tragedies and hard turns. He was an aristocrat, but no feather-bed aristocrat.

Dabney the Magnificent

It should be obvious from the preceding overview, but let us say it again: Dabney was a *remarkably* gifted man. Perhaps this can be made plain by putting some of his accomplishments in one place, all in a row. He was a great theologian, a powerful preacher, a successful farmer, a builder of two houses, a maker of his own furniture, a poet, a biographer, a skilled mechanic, an architect, a surveyor, an inventor and holder of some patents, a political economist, and a trusted military adjutant to one of the greatest generals in the history of warfare. About the only thing that Dabney was not was photogenic.

Dabney's wife was related to Stonewall Jackson's wife, and at the beginning of the war, Dabney served the Confederate Army as chaplain during the summer of 1861, when he did not have to teach. This kind of thing was done by others as well. For example, the great classicist Basil Gildersleeve at Johns Hopkins in Baltimore would teach during the school year and spend his summers fighting for the Confederacy.

As Dabney was doing this same thing, he got a bad case of camp fever and had to return home. A year later, Stonewall Jackson wrote to request that Dabney consider becoming his Chief-of-Staff. Dabney went to see Jackson with the goal of persuading him from this great madness, and to accept his renewed service as chaplain instead. Jackson overruled Dabney's objections, gave him two days to read a book on warfare, and then installed him.[3]

At the beginning the other soldiers made fun of Dabney (because of his customs of dress and his umbrella), but his abilities soon enough won their respect. Stonewall helped to cure Dabney of his dressing habits one rainy day by saying to his men, Dabney among them, "Gentlemen, let us ride!" Off they went at a full gallop, and when they were done, Dabney's umbrella was in tatters, and he was soon outfitted differently. He gained the respect of the other soldiers quite swiftly.[4]

3. Johnson, *Dabney*, 236, 243, 261ff.
4. Ibid., 270.

Initially one Colonel Grigsby said this when asked about the new adjutant: "I concluded that old Jack must be a fatalist sure enough, when he put in an Ironside Presbyterian parson as his chief of staff, but I have bright hopes of headquarters, seeing they are no longer omniscient." Just a few weeks later, Grigsby said of Dabney, "Our parson is not afraid of Yankee bullets, and I tell you he preaches like hell."[5] We have countless preachers in our day whose preaching could be described in just the same way, but in our day it is not a compliment.

Dabney was with Stonewall during the great Valley Campaign— April to June of 1862. He was invaluable to Stonewall and on at least one occasion he single-handedly averted a military disaster by saving Jackson's ammunition train. When Dabney wrote about this incident in his biography of Stonewall, he wrote himself out of the account by putting his role in the third person. When asked about it many years after the war, he admitted that he was the officer who had saved Jackson's reserve ammunition supply.

This is how it happened. Because of a blunder by Jackson's cavalry, Federal troops surprised Jackson and his staff at a place called Port Republic. Stonewall's ammunition trains were coming across a bridge into the town. When surprised, Jackson got away back over the bridge with part of his staff, galloping at full speed. Two of his staff were captured by the Federals, and Dabney escaped in another direction—not back across the bridge with Jackson. It quickly became apparent that the Federals were going to capture the ammunition convoy, but on his side of the bridge Dabney rounded up about fifteen riflemen, a small band of artillerymen, and then about twenty-five cavalrymen (who had been on picket duty) and set up a stiff resistance that saved Jackson's ammunition from capture until Jackson could organize a counter-attack and retake the town.[6]

At another battle, a battle at Gaines' Mill, Dabney performed an essential service for Jackson, turning an almost disaster into

5. Ibid., 264.
6. Ibid., 265ff.

a splendid victory. He did this without informing Jackson of his own role in it, and so the credit went undiscovered until much later. Jackson had entrusted an incompetent staff officer with orders to send reserves into battle, which he entirely bungled and did not do. Dabney had protested giving this responsibility to the incompetent officer, and then later went after the reserves that this man was keeping out of the battle and sent six of the best brigades into the thick of it, late in the afternoon, saving the battle. Dabney was a gifted military officer, and he had become one in a matter of weeks.[7]

Unfortunately, Dabney had to resign, again because of camp fever. Stonewall told Dr. Samuel Morrison that he considered Dabney the most efficient officer he knew. Given everything we know about Dabney's extraordinary competence elsewhere, and what we know about Stonewall's military genius and insight, this should not be taken as hyperbole. It was high praise indeed.

Clear and Blurred Vision

With a man like this it is tempting to overlook his faults, but given Dabney's commitment to Scripture, this would be the one thing he would insist we *not* do. A century or more has given a better perspective (on *some* things), and one of those things is the matter of racism. Although prior to the war, Dabney should be numbered among those who were agitating to reform the treatment of blacks in the South, it has to be said that this reformer's zeal was mingled with what we would today identify as racism. Too many Christians in the South, Dabney included, identified the cultural divide between Europe and Africa as a divide necessitated by "the very nature of things." Even so, Dabney (along with most Southern apologists) was adamantly opposed to the popular scientific view of *polygenesis*, a theory which held that whites and blacks were entirely differently species. The racism of the North was virulent, scientific, modern, and cruel. The racism of the South was just as sinful, but

7. Ibid., 267ff.

it was a different kind of sin—paternalistic, opportunistic, and condescending.

After the fall of the Confederacy, Dabney's aristocratic views of society were continually insulted, and his views developed a bitter edge, a bitterness not evident before the war. In one of his essays, he even comes close to acknowledging this personal element out loud. After the war, Dabney was still agitating for honest and kind treatment of the freed slaves, but this is clearly mingled with a condescending racism and a hard edge of rhetoric concerning the limited capacities of blacks.

It would be easy enough to give you some quotations from Dabney which would illustrate this view of race, a view that none of us here would want to be associated with. I refrain from doing so only because our opponents in this controversy are being led by liars, cheats, incompetents, and scoundrels. It would be very easy for them to say that "Douglas Wilson honored Dabney in his lecture, quoted Dabney to the following effect, and don't you all see that Dabney is his hero?" So I will simply acknowledge this unfortunate and sinful element in Dabney's thinking, an element that even went so far as (in his *Systematic Theology*) to chastise redheads who did not understand their innate inferiority.

So I will content myself with condemning a quotation from the most famous white supremacist (to use our current phrase for this) of the nineteenth century, a gentleman named Abraham Lincoln. He said, "I have no purpose to introduce political and social equality between the white and black races . . . inasmuch as it becomes a necessity that there must be a difference, I, as well as Judge Douglas, am in favor of the race to which I belong having the superior position. I have never said anything to the contrary."[8]

Let this condemnation here serve as a condemnation of this view, and any view similar to it. I condemn the racism of R. L. Dabney, of Margaret Sanger, of Abraham Lincoln, of Charles Darwin, of Louis Farrakhan, and of Ted Kennedy. This enthusiastic

---

8. Thomas DiLorenzo, *The Real Lincoln: A New Look at Abraham Lincoln, His Agenda, and an Unnecessary War* (Roseville: Prima Publishing, 2002), 11.

condemnation cheerfully includes all the inhabitants of the right-wing fever swamps, the overt white supremacists of the glazed-eye crowd. My view of the so-called conservative white supremacists that disfigure the political landscape today can be summed up in just one little joke: "What is most effective pick-up line at white supremacist conventions?" "I don't know, what is it?" "'Hey, nice tooth.'"

Here is Dabney, in a letter to Major General Howard, who was the chief of the Freedman's Bureau after the war.

> When I claim that the South did thus much for the Africans, I am far from boasting. We ought to have done much more. Instead of pointing to it with self-laudation, it becomes us, with profound humility towards God, to confess our shortcomings toward our servants. He has been pleased, in His sovereign and fearful dispensation, to lay upon us a grievous affliction, and we know He is too just to do this except for our sins. While I am as certain as the sure word of Scripture can make me concerning any principle of social duty, that there was nothing sinful in the relation of master and slave itself, I can easily believe that our failure to fulfill some of the duties of that relation is among the sins for which God's hand now makes us smart. And it does not become those who are under His discipline to boast of their good works. No; verily we have sinned; my argument is that you must do more for the negro than we sinners of the South have done.[9]

Dabney was nothing if not insightful, and when someone as clear-headed and logical as he was finds himself surrounded by a victorious wickedness, a vicious insolence, and a confederacy of dunces—in short, the Intoleristas of his day—an ever-present temptation is that of becoming hard and bitter. Dabney was too warm a man to be embittered throughout the course of his life, but it has to be said that his political views on race relations hardened after the war, and that there was a bitterness here that marred his legacy. That bitterness led him to fight to keep the Presbyterian Church lily-white at the end of the war, and the worst thing about

9. Dabney, *Discussions: Secular*, 32.

this was the fact that Dabney argued from expedience and not from Scripture. It was not like him at all. As Eugene Genovese mentioned in a piece of private correspondence, it was a "terrible moment." But even in the midst of that bitterness, it must be remembered that he continued to fight for better treatment of the freed blacks.

His Death

Dabney died peacefully at home on the third of January, 1898. He had been anticipating his death and spent time working around the house to make it more suitable for his wife to live there alone. In his last years, one of the things he wrote was this charge to his sons and daughters and their children.

> I desire before I leave the world, as my best legacy to my family, my serious, solemn advice, to make choice of God for their God. He has been my father's God, and the God of your mother's predecessors. I solemnly charge you to make it your first care to seek after peace with God, and being reconciled, to make it your study to please God in all things.
>
> Wait diligently upon the means of grace, attending the worship of God in his house; study the Word, after secret prayer, especially family and the public ordinances.
>
> Beware of the mere form of these duties; but cry to the Lord for communion with him, so that you may worship him in spirit and in truth.
>
> Follow God fully, without turning aside. I have often devoted all of you to God, and there is nothing I have so much at heart as this: that you may indeed be the Lord's; and if you turn aside from this way, I will have this as a witness against you in the day of the Lord.
>
> Be good to your mother, as you would have God's blessing. She will need your comfort. Beware of religion that is most taken up with public matters.
>
> The sum of the gospel is Christ crucified. I commit my body to the dust, hoping and expecting the spirit will in due time quicken my mortal body. My spirit I commit to my Lord Jesus Christ; to him I have entrusted it long ago.

Now, my dear boys, this is my last legacy, that we all meet where there is no more death, sorrow nor sin.

Your devoted father, R. L. Dabney

Then there are two quotations for a postscript:

"Be kindly affectionate one to another."
"Remember the Sabbath day to keep it holy."[10]

Clear Vision

Dabney is valuable because he was a man who thought in terms of *principles*. When I first started reading him, I was struck by the many passages that were virtually prophetic. Here are just three examples.

But nearly all public men and divines declare that the State schools are the glory of America, that they are a finality, and in no event to be surrendered. And we have seen that their complete secularization is logically inevitable. Christians must prepare themselves then, for the following results: All prayers, catechisms, and Bibles will ultimately be driven out of the schools.[11]

[Northern conservatism] is a party which never conserves anything. Its history has been that it demurs to each aggression of the progressive party, and aims to save its credit by a respectable amount of growling, but always acquiesces at last in the innovation . . . American conservatism is merely the shadow that follows Radicalism as it moves forward towards perdition.[12]

There are those . . . who exclaim: "Let us bury the dead past. Its issues are all antiquated, and of no more practical significance. . . ." I rejoin: Be sure that the former issues are really dead before you bury them.[13]

10. Johnson, *Dabney*, 523.
11. Dabney, "Secularized Education" in *Discussions: Secular*, 242.
12. Dabney, "Women's Rights Women" in ibid., 496.
13. Dabney, "The New South" in ibid., 20.

Before You Bury Them

Throughout the course of his life, Dabney served two causes, one of them temporal and the other eternal. The temporal cause was a lost cause, and although Dabney's allegiance to and affection for that cause remained to the end of his life, he did acknowledge that it was, in the Providence of God, a *lost* cause. This is a truth we also acknowledge. In one sense, the antebellum South was a Christian nation, but it was a Christian nation that invited, and *received*, a genuinely severe judgment from the God who is not mocked. This judgment from a holy God included all the atrocities of Sherman, and sinful men must always bow before the judgments of the Almighty and turn to the Scriptures to learn how to accept those judgments. A man will reap what he sows, and so do nations. Dabney was convinced that a holy God commanded that the South fall, and that she fall because of her sins. This is basic to covenantal thinking.

This being the case, we here in the United States today should hear the Word of God and tremble. If God does this sort of thing, in time and in history, what will He do with a nation such as ours? We are hostile to the poor and needy, fattening federal bureaucrats so long as they pretend to cry in the name of the poor. We have murdered over forty million infants since the infamous *Roe v. Wade* decision. We are about to have sodomite marriage imposed on us through the full faith and credit clause of the Constitution. Massachusetts has mandated it, and after the inevitable court scuffles, we will find ourselves living in far more than five cities of the plain. From shore to shore, we will continue to grow our amber waves of stain. What shall we do? How shall we as Christians live?

R. L. Dabney was also a faithful servant to another cause, an eternal cause, and this cause is by no means lost. In the one hundred and six years since Dabney's death, the Christian faith has exploded all around the globe. Countless millions have believed in Jesus Christ since Dabney went to be with Jesus Christ. Africa is rapidly becoming Christian. China is rapidly becoming Christian. Through gates of pearl streams in a countless host.

God the Father has promised all the nations to the Lord Jesus Christ, and God will fulfill all these promises. He will do this in one of two ways. Nations that persist in defying Him will fall under His temporal judgments. In this category, we may consider the examples provoked by the hubris of the former Soviet Union and Nazi Germany.

But there is another way to fall under the judgment, a far more merciful way, and that is when we fall under the judgment of God in the cross of Jesus Christ. When Jesus Christ died on the cross, all in union with Him died there as well, under the judgment of God. When Jesus died, we died. When Jesus was buried, we were buried. When Jesus rose, we rose from the dead. When Jesus ascended into heaven, and was seated at the right hand of God the Father, He was seated on a throne *from which He cannot be removed*. His crown rights, established in heaven, by definition cannot be a lost cause. He has inherited all the nations of men from the river to the ends of the earth. This means that every vain hope that sets itself up against the knowledge of God in the face of Christ is the lost cause. Sin is the lost cause. Vanity of mind is the lost cause. Autonomy is the lost cause. The sixties are the lost cause. Secularism is the lost cause. Secular unbelief is the lost cause. Ecclesiastical unbelief is the lost cause. The Enlightenment is the lost cause.

God has exalted Jesus Christ and has given Him the name that is above every name, that at the name of Jesus every knee shall bow, whether in heaven, or on earth, or under the earth. Every knee shall bow, whether inside the Student Union Building or outside of it. Every knee shall bow, whether American or Chinese. Every knee shall bow, whether in Massachusetts or Alabama. Every knee shall bow, whether holding political office or not. This is God's agenda for the world: He sent His Son into the world, not in order to condemn the world, but rather to save it.

Now for the secularists who read or hear these words, this is no doubt a *scary* agenda. But is this a political agenda? *God forbid!* Why would we use the grimy little god of politics to try to usher in what

Jesus Christ already purchased on the cross with His own blood? Why would we insult His authority in this unbelieving way?

But do we have an agenda *for* politics? Yes, we do. The Christian faith is public. Like all other sinful things in this world, Jesus Christ offers politics salvation. But when Jesus Christ invites anyone or anything to Himself, He bids him come and die. So this cannot be salvation through self-effort, self-righteousness, or self-importance. It cannot be through men pretending to be little divinities, bossing everyone else into their Enlightenment categories. It cannot be through the inherent intolerance of the diversity-or-else crowd, those who love diversity until they actually see some of it.

In bringing this about, we do not use the instruments of campaigns, petitions, or other forms of petty coercion in order to bring in the kingdom of our Lord and of His Christ. The instruments we use—because these are the only instruments assigned to us—are the means of grace. We receive the waters of death to self, the waters of baptism, we worship the Lord Jesus in a weekly commemoration of His conquest of death, we sing psalms and hymns, we hear the Scriptures read, we hear the Word preached, and we gladly partake of the Lord's Supper every week. *This* is how Jesus Christ will inherit all the nations of the earth. *This* is how the idols of secularism will topple. *This* is how the Enlightenment will fall, like Dagon in that Philistine temple.

Our God reigns—yesterday, today, and forever—and so long as He reigns, we as His people (together with Dabney) can never serve a lost cause. The Christian faith is public, and not private. It is the salvation of the world, and the world can no more evade that salvation than a deserted lawn chair on the beach can resist a tsunami—even if the Styrofoam cooler comes over to help. Do you want to stop the salvation of the world that Jesus purchased? You might better spend your time throwing snowballs at the sun.

So do the secularists have cause to worry? Yes, they most certainly do. But they do not need to worry because we Christians have picked up their weapons of petty politics. They rather need to worry because in repentance we have *dropped* such weapons, and in holy congregations we have begun to worship God the Father through Jesus Christ, in the power of the Holy Spirit. As we glorify the name of Jesus Christ in heaven, we are asking God to glorify the name of Jesus Christ on earth, for we are asking that His will be done on earth as it is in heaven. That petition has been granted, is being granted, and shall be granted. Glory to God, who has visited this sorry world with His great salvation, our Lord Jesus Christ, world without end. Amen.

8.

Fragments from the Controversy

The following excerpts are taken from a paper circulated in a private discussion with a Christian historian, Dr. Tracy McKenzie, who differs strongly with me on some of the central points in this discussion. Since some of the points made in our exchange should be of interest generally, I have included them here. I have removed some of the personal interaction and some material used elsewhere. Despite our sharp disagreement on this subject, I want to note here that I have the highest respect for his personal and professional integrity and am genuinely grateful to him. To adjust a proverbial saying from Emeth in The Last Battle, *a noble friend is the best gift from the gods, and a noble adversary is the next best.*

Logical Failures

Dr. McKenzie makes the point that once we have shown that the Bible does not automatically condemn slavery as something *malum in se*, for us to turn to an assessment of Southern slavery is a "logical leap." He says, quite rightly, that helping Christians understand the biblical teaching on slavery "does not require that they arrive at a positive assessment of slavery in *any particular historical context*." Of course it does not. The Bible could teach what it does about slavery, and Southern slave-owners could have all been a cross between orcs and Klingons, and the Bible would still be true, and the evil slave-owners condemned by what the Scriptures require. It is certainly true that the Bible's defense of godly slave-owning cannot be twisted into a defense of *ungodly* slave-owning. We are not denying this principle—rather, the bulk of our booklet testifies that we agree with this point. The treatment of slaves in the ante-bellum South is a post-Scripture historical question that Scripture does not address.

So why do we want to defend the Southern setting at all, to any extent? The answer to that is supplied in the booklet, and it is an argument that McKenzie obviously did not follow. Because of the *way* slavery was ended, we are dealing with atrocious consequences down to the present. How many millions of unborn children have died because federal authorities determined that the Constitution is a blank screen on which they may project their desires? When did this process start in a significant way? When did the Constitution become this nose of wax?

McKenzie says this: *"the entire discussion of the treatment of Southern slaves is utterly unnecessary to accomplish the purposes the authors espouse."* This simply shows that he was unable to follow the argument on pages 9–11, and it was a plain argument, plainly stated. Because McKenzie is an intelligent, Christian man, this is why I believe we are playing a minor version of what I call "paradigm bumper cars." Our point is not to defend obedience to the Bible's teaching on slavery in some abstract, utopian setting. The point was to defend the Bible as a book to be obeyed completely, in the midst of the messy and sinful realities that human beings create for themselves. The Bible is to be obeyed by us now in our current culture wars, and the Bible was to have been obeyed a century and a half ago by us in our nineteenth-century culture wars. Our argument is that our earlier disobedi-ence is a central part of what is driving our current disobedience. McKenzie is free to disagree with this argument, but this section of his article shows that he has not understood it.

Few Rebellions?

McKenzie rejects our argument that if the treatment of slaves had been as horrendous as claimed by the abolitionists, then there should have been far more abolitionists and far more slave rebel-lions. McKenzie does not find this argument compelling, which is fine, but it should be noted that since this is a counterfactual argument (as he points out), this should be categorized as a simple disagreement between us. But he says, "The same argument, incidentally—that few uprisings imply contentment—could also be employed to defend communist rule in China, the reign of the Taliban in Afghanistan, and the benevolence of S.S. guards in Nazi concentration camps." This kind of reply illustrates yet again how he is taking our background assumptions and construing them in a negative way for rhetorical effect. But there is a reply.

In order to avoid uprisings, the communists in China had to murder millions of people. The slaves in Haiti (whose conditions were far worse than those of their counterparts in the South) did rise up in a bloody way. Our argument is simply an assertion that the many observers who traveled through the South were not like Lenin's "useful idiots" who went to the Soviet Union and saw peace and harmony everywhere, instead of the genocide that they ought to have seen. The South was not covered with death camps of the variety found so popular in the twentieth century. If the situation was as evil across the board as some have described it, there would have been far more revolts (as in Haiti), or true totalitarian measures would have been necessary to head off such revolts. As McKenzie points out, this is a counterfactual argument, but it certainly seems to me something that a reasonable and historically-informed person could believe.

At the same time, it is important to note again that this is a *comparative* situation. There *were* slave revolts in the South, and they were brutally put down. From Eugene Genovese: "In 1856 the slaveholders of Tennessee repeated the performance with a slight variation: They carried the impaled heads in a parade. And unlike the Louisianians of 1811, they had not even confronted slaves in arms; their victims had only fallen under suspicion of insurrectionary design."[1] But at the same time, Genovese still notes the "infrequency and low intensity of revolts in the Old South relative to those elsewhere."[2]

I. Eugene Genovese, *From Rebellion to Revolution* (Baton Rouge: Louisiana State Univ. Press, 1979), 106–107.

2. Ibid., xxii.

In the same book, he points to a number of contributing factors to this comparative reality; I simply want to argue that the presence of a genuine Christian ethos in the Old South was one of them.[3]

Straw Man

Another related device that McKenzie uses in his argumentation is this one. I said in a letter to him that I had been influenced by the work of Richard Weaver on the Southern intellectual tradition. He then obtained a couple of quotations from Weaver's book (his selection, not mine), quotations that are easy enough to refute—with the intimation being made that these passages (or others like them) were what I was talking about. It is like telling someone that I am Jeffersonian in my views, and having them conclude that I am talking about sex with a woman named Sally Hemmings instead of a favorable view of decentralized government. Why didn't McKenzie take *this* quotation from Weaver instead?

> The precarious state of our civilization has grown with our control over nature, though we were promised an opposite result . . . everywhere crassness, moral obtuseness, and degradation are on the increase.[4]

Maybe it was *this* sort of thing I was talking about. But McKenzie didn't check with me, and just went off to find an embarrassing quotation. This is not how we should be debating with each other.

Real Plagiarism

McKenzie also defends the historians' guild against our charge that they (as a rule) exhibit conformity to the current *kultursmog*, and he

---

3. This last paragraph was not part of my original response to McKenzie, and as Dr. Genovese was kind enough to point out that my original response to McKenzie was weak at this point, I have added this clarification.

4. Weaver, *The Southern Tradition at Bay*, 15. By the way, in this section, McKenzie gets the title of the book right, but in several other places he calls it *The Southern Intellectual Tradition at Bay*.

is dismissive of our critique of them as overwhelmingly conforming to an anti-Christian worldview.

There is a way for us to test this scientifically. Let us take something of a historical nature, one that is factually indisputable but which conflicts with the current canons of correctness. A good example of this would be the massive plagiarism evident throughout Martin Luther King, Jr.'s doctoral thesis, submitted to Boston University. McKenzie should get a copy of the book which documents this completely[5] and then simply write a chatty letter to his colleagues in the history department at Behemoth University, recommending the book. He should make sure he signs this letter, and make sure that it is on BU stationery. Actually, there is no need to risk anything; we can do all this in a thought experiment. We all know that on certain subjects (like this one), *the historical facts do not matter*, not even to most historians. I simply believe that in any modern discussion of antebellum slavery, anyone who takes a position that maintains that the conditions of Southern slavery were more benign than we thought has to be prepared for the same kind of treatment.

Things Not Said

Our monograph was only thirty-nine pages, and McKenzie's article is twenty-three pages. In such a short compass, no one can cover everything, anticipate everything, or cite everything. But more than once McKenzie treats omissions as having some culpable purpose behind them. For example, he says, "This finding leaves a rather different impression in our minds, doesn't it? Why did Wilson and Wilkins leave it out?"

But why in his treatment of the scholarly sloppiness of *Time on the Cross* does he neglect to mention that one of the authors is a Nobel laureate? And why, when he was addressing how we have made ourselves vulnerable to plausible charges of racism, did McKenzie neglect to point out that we published *The Biblical Offense of Racism* at

5. Theodore Pappas, *Plagiarism and the Culture War* (Tampa: Hallberg Publishing, 1998). In the foreword, Eugene Genovese said that "this brave book deserves a wide reading."

the same time that we published *Southern Slavery as It Was*? Why did he not mention my debate with a white racialist in the same issue of *Credenda* from which he cites another article, a debate which I mentioned in my letter to him? I am happy to believe that it was because his article was only twenty-three pages long, and you can't say everything. But the omissions *did* strengthen the case he was trying to make. If this is bad, then why did he do it? If it is okay, then why does he object when we did?

Real Southern Problems

What we actually said in our booklet about *the very real problems* in the South bears repeating. Among a number of other similar comments, we said,

> The point of this small booklet is to establish that this impression [of Southern slavery as unbridled evil] is largely false. It is important to note, however, that the impression is not *entirely* false. The truth is, Southern slavery is open to criticism because it did not follow the biblical pattern at every point. Some of the state laws regulating slavery could not be defended biblically (the laws forbidding the teaching of reading and writing, for example). One cannot defend the abuse some slaves had to endure. None can excuse the immorality some masters and overseers indulged in with some slave women. The separation of families that sometimes occurred was deplorable. These were sad realities in the Southern system. Our purpose here is *not* to defend any such practices—where and when they occurred. We have no interest in defending the racism (in both the North and the South) which was often seen as the basic justification for the system, and we do in fact condemn it most heartily.[6]

At the end of this passage, we footnote *The Biblical Offense of Racism*, also published by Canon Press at the same time. Not only were we not interested in defending racism, we were interested in *attacking* it. A little later, we said, "We have no concern to whitewash the sins of the South—or the North for that matter. Where there is

6. Wilson and Wilkins, *Southern Slavery*, 7–8.

sin, let us freely confess and forsake it."[7] Other passages repeat this position:

> It is obvious that in a fallen world, an institution like slavery will be accompanied by many attendant evils. Such evils existed with ancient Hebrew slavery, ancient Roman slavery, and with American slavery.[8]

> We must reject the childish mentality which seeks to engage in mindless partisanship at the expense of truth. All attempts to say that the North represented nothing good, and that the South contained nothing sinful are examples of this kind of infantilism. R. L. Dabney, a godly man who fought for the South, made the point that the South lost the war *because she was under the judgment of God.* . . . And although the South was correct about the central issues of that war, southern diehards must learn the hard lesson of Habakkuk, who had to accept that God can use an ungodly nation to judge another nation which is "not as bad" (Hab. 1:13).[9]

> Slavery *was* attended with many evils. As it existed in the South, it was not in any way perfect or utopian. But too often the *real* problems with slavery were not the problems we have been told about. However, as discussed earlier, Christians should be quick to notice the discrepancies between biblical slavery and that practiced in the South. These differences between the biblical standard and Southern slavery do make impossible an unqualified defense of the institution as it existed and operated in the South. Furthermore, the cruel mistreatment given to some slaves is inexcusable and truly despicable. All such evil was wicked and indefensible.[10]

> None need lament the passing of slavery. But who cannot but lament the damage to both white and black that has occurred as a consequence of the *way* it was abolished?[11]

7. Ibid., 8.
8. Ibid., 10.
9. Ibid., 13.
10. Ibid., 35–36.
11. Ibid., 39.

In the light of all this, McKenzie says, "Wilson and Wilkins do not defend the disruption of slave marriages, but neither do they attach the significance to the practice that many Southern Presbyterians did. To Wilson and Wilkins, the problem was apparently incidental; men like Thornwell believed it threatened to invalidate the entire institution." Now, what part of the word *deplorable* did McKenzie not understand? Far from believing this to be an "incidental" problem, I actually believe that it is one of the reasons why a just and holy God visited such a fierce destruction upon the South. What happened to the South, Sherman and all, was deserved by the South. God did not waste that region of the country because they had been playing too much gin rummy. When we said that the injustices perpetrated in the South were the cause of God bringing a severe judgment upon her, *we really believe it.*

Please remember that throughout our booklet, in describing features of Southern slavery, we used words like *deplorable, wicked, evil, despicable, cruel, inexcusable, abuse, immorality,* and, following Dabney, *criminal barbarity.* Now here is a simple Golden Rule question. Would anyone who had *not* read our booklet, but who had read McKenzie's article about it, gotten *this* impression of what we really believe (and plainly said) about such things? The answer is *no.* So why should I believe that he has special competence in representing Southerners who have been dead for more than a century, *when I know for a fact* that he has grossly misrepresented *this* Southerner, despite the fact that I went out of my way to condemn in round numbers every Southern sin I could think of?

Amazingly Benign

This is the context in which we should consider the following comment about us: "Wilson and Wilkins make two such broad generalizations. The first is that slave life was 'amazingly benign.'" McKenzie then goes on to discuss something which we were not discussing at all when we made this comment. He brings up the separation of slave families, which we had already condemned *as deplorable,* and then rhetorically asks, "This qualifies as 'amazingly benign'?"

In using the phrase "amazingly benign," a fair approach would link it to another phrase, which would be "compared to what?" We were not arguing that it was benign to separate a slave family as compared to keeping that slave family together. A fair-minded reading of our booklet would show that we would say antebellum slavery was "amazingly benign" as compared to (1) the rhetoric of the abolitionists; (2) what was occurring in other parts of the new world that used slaves, such as Haiti or Brazil; and (3) what had happened in other slave-owning societies in ancient history, like pagan Rome.[12] If McKenzie had wanted to, he could have completed his argument by showing that Wilson and Wilkins believe that "deplorable" conditions are "amazingly benign." Then we would have really looked silly.

If at First You Don't Secede . . .

A good portion of McKenzie's section on the League of the South has the effect of making any desire for secession for cultural reasons look ludicrous. Now I am not a member of the League, and Steve has recently resigned from the board of directors because his priorities have been shifting. But let me say this to support the League (mildly), even though I do differ with them. I am not a member of the League because I believe that the *severe* problems this nation has do not admit of a political or cultural solution. There is no way out for us apart from a massive reformation of liturgy and doctrine in the evangelical church nationwide. That is where I want to concentrate all my energies, and that is what I understand Steve as also wanting to do. I believe that the League's attempts to stop what is happening are in the same category as the attempts being made by Focus on the Family to get prayer back in the government schools.

But let me defend them to this extent. They do not want to maintain a distinct Southern heritage because they are afraid that some Yankee judge will outlaw grits. Please note *where we actually*

12. For example, see Jennifer Glancy, *Slavery in Early Christianity* (Oxford: Oxford Univ. Press, 2002), 1–49.

are as a nation—just a few weeks away from the full faith and credit clause of the mangled Constitution, courtesy of Massachusetts, being used to impose homosexual marriages on Alabama, Virginia, Idaho, and all the cities of the plain. Secession over such a cause is impossible (because of the current impotence of the church). But if the church were *not* impotent, and if a state were able to successfully secede from the Union rather than have such an abomination imposed upon them, it would be entirely noble. Not only would it be worth doing, it would be *obligatory*.

But the League of the South should not be anticipating large successes in their fight for traditional culture because the carrier of all culture is *cultus*, the worship of God. Because our general evangelical *cultus* is both inane and idolatrous, there will be no salvaging of our culture in the next few weeks. The reformation of the church is what we need to be eating, drinking, and breathing—all the time. As for the folks in the League of the South and Focus on the Family, God bless them. I wish them the best, and I understand why they want to get out there and make a direct challenge to the abortion culture, the homosexual culture, and so forth. But they will fail because so many Christians still refuse to place the sign of Christ's ownership on their babies, refuse to bring them up in the nurture and admonition of the Lord, refuse to teach them the glories of celebrating the Lord's Day, and refuse to conduct their worship services as though our triune God is holy, holy, actually holy.

Many of the folks in the League are good diagnosticians. But they are not actively pushing the remedy, which will only be found if judgment begins with the household of God.

Racism

We have a thoroughly integrated congregation here at Christ Church—probably more so than numerous secular organizations around our white little town. More than that, many of our families are mixed race families. Nevertheless, McKenzie worries that our views might prove to be a stumbling block. If our teaching presents a stumbling block to black Christians, and other ethnic Christians, we certainly have not noticed it. Steve's church in Monroe is integrated, *and ours is markedly so.*

When we said in our booklet that it is racist to say that black men as a class could be cowed to such an extent that they would not defend their women, McKenzie takes issue with this by appealing to a *tight* definition of racism. He says, "'racism' imputes genetic differences to a racial group, differences that transcend time and cultural circumstance," and I agree with this definition. But then when he is criticizing us for opening ourselves up to plausible accusations of racism, the definition broadens considerably. This is using different weights and measures. If racism is what McKenzie says, then by no stretch of the imagination could we be plausibly accused of being racist. But then McKenzie wants to say that we have culpably set ourselves up to be plausibly accused of being racist. However, we deny emphatically any genetic inferiority in blacks, and hold that to maintain genetic inferiority of blacks is unbiblical and un-Christian. In the booklet, we had a substantive discussion that showed this clearly. We pointed to the universal redemption of Christ (Rev. 5:9–10), the integrated leadership of the church at Antioch (Acts 13:1), and that Moses married a black woman (Num. 12).[13]

McKenzie says that we cannot defend the South without inviting this charge, and he says it is hard for us to answer because our behavior made such a charge plausible. He says, "in the antebellum South slavery and racism were inextricably intertwined, and to posit a separate existence for either is ahistorical."

But we are not positing a separate existence for the two *back then*. We are positing a separate existence for them in *our* thinking. A century later, we have a better perspective on some things than they did, and we believe that racism is a sin to be repented of. But we do not believe that for Virginia to think she had the right of secession because she had expressly reserved that right to herself when she ratified the Constitution (as also did Rhode Island and New York) is a sin to be repented of as well. We do not think it was a

13. Wilson and Wilkins, *Southern Slavery,* 14.

sin (*malum in se*) to own slaves, provided they were treated scriptur-
ally—as that old cotton planter the apostle Paul once taught. And
we did maintain, following the Scriptures, that the slave trade was
an abomination.

But notice how McKenzie is using different weights and measures again. Not only was the historical practice of slavery all
bound up with racism, *so was abolitionism.* Virtually no one, North
or South, was free of this contagion. The cause of the South was
afflicted with racism. So was the cause of the North. The Southern
Christians did better than most others because they at least fought
for the understanding that blacks were men. They were frequently
and erroneously thought to be inferior men, but *men* nonetheless.
The accepted science of the day was arguing for polygenesis, the
theory that maintained whites and blacks were two different species. We repudiate all such thinking.

For the sake of evangelizing or discipling modern blacks, is it
really necessary for me to start praising Abraham Lincoln, who really was a forthright white supremacist? Here is honest Abe:

> I have no purpose to introduce political and social equality be-
> tween the white and black races . . . inasmuch as it becomes a neces-
> sity that there must be a difference, I, as well as Judge Douglas, am
> in favor of the race to which I belong having the superior position.
> I have never said anything to the contrary.[14]

All racism is to be rejected with loathing. The North needed
to repent of one kind of racism and the South needed to repent
of another kind. But in the Southern form, there was more for a
Christian preacher to work with (faith in Scripture), which means
there was a more obvious way to call them to repentance. Genovese
notes, "Scientific racists, who asserted the biological inferiority of
blacks, scoffed at the suggestion that they could progress to freedom, but the Southern divines despised the scientific racists."[15] *As*

14. DiLorenzo, *The Real Lincoln*, 11.
15. Genovese, *A Consuming Fire*, 76.

do I. It is true that I have great sympathies for Dabney, and this makes me suspect in McKenzie's eyes. But I am in the same place as Genovese on this, who has the same kind of sympathy for a very great man. But I do not honor Dabney (or the many others like him) in his faults, and racism is among those faults. Even Mark Noll, whom McKenzie quotes approvingly, makes this distinction between their exegesis on slavery (which was solid and compelling) and their "common sense" assumptions about race, which were so much flapdoodle.

McKenzie says that it is historically untenable to separate racism from the cause of the South. But it is just as untenable to separate it from the cause of the North.

Better Off

We lamented not the passing of slavery, but rather the *way* it was ended. This baffles McKenzie, who asks, "logically, doesn't this imply that the United States, at least collectively, was better off with slavery than it now is without it?"

Think for a moment. How many millions of children have been dismembered in the last thirty years? What legal principles did *Roe v. Wade* rest upon? And when were *those* principles established? It is my conviction that if we had ended slavery in a *way* that kept the Constitution intact, it would not have been possible for the Supreme Court to overturn the laws of virtually every state in the Union which outlawed abortion.

When McKenzie assumes that "we" are better off today, is he counting the unborn or not? Perhaps we should just limit this question to children in the wombs of *black* women today. If you were a black fetus in Atlanta, Georgia, what were your odds of ever seeing the light of day in 1858? What are your odds in 2005? A lot of kids died back then, but not because the vile democracy they had the misfortune to be conceived in had somehow taken to the belief that to suck someone else's brains out with a vacuum cleaner was a high and noble *constitutional right*. When and how did the Constitution come to mean *that?* McKenzie rejects our answer. Perhaps he would like to supply a different one.

So here it is. No, *we are not better off.* We murder lots and lots of people, just like Stalin, Pol Pot, Hitler, and Mao did. On the bright side, we have lots of flat screen plasma televisions and cell phones readily available.

What the War Was Over

McKenzie quotes us as saying the war was over the biblical meaning of constitutional government, and interprets us as thinking that all the Southern leaders were biblical Christians, going to war for the text of Scripture. But this is not what we were saying at all. We acknowledged that neither side was monolithic[16] and we said that "*by the time of the war,* the intellectual *leadership* of the South was conservative, orthodox, and Christian."[17] We were not maintaining that the South was a postmillennial paradise. Of course it was not. But the leadership of the North exhibited the marks of a different religion than that of the South. Just one example of military leadership should make part of this point:

> The most influential Christian soldiers were invariably acknowledged to be Southerners. Several Confederate corps commanders, such as Jeb Stuart, D. H. Hill, and John B. Gordon, were celebrated for their outstanding piety. Episcopal clergymen Leonidas Polk and William Nelson Pendleton exercised great authority and influence throughout the war. The three major army leaders in the western theater, Braxton Bragg, Joseph E. Johnston, and John Bell Hood, were all converted during the period of the army revivals. And, of course, Robert E. Lee and Stonewall Jackson of the Army of Northern Virginia were thought to epitomize the highest ideals of military valor and personal sanctity. Churchmen in both the North and the South praised these generals as exemplars of American piety.[18]

16. Wilson and Wilkins, *Southern Slavery,* 12.
17. Ibid., 12. Emphasis added this time around.
18. Gardiner Shattuck, Jr., *A Shield and Hiding Place: The Religious Life of the Civil War Armies* (Macon: Mercer Univ. Press, 1987), 105.

When I say this sort of thing—that the North had drifted into theologically liberal goo-thought and the South was orthodox and Christian—I know I am painting with a broad brush. I know it is a *generalization*. Even today, if I were to refer to the "Bible Belt," I would not consider myself refuted if someone went hunting and triumphantly found seven atheistic freethinkers in Shreveport. But as generalizations go, it is still quite fair. Here is another example of another historian doing just what we did:

> The religiously orthodox Old South, in contradistinction to the religiously liberal Northeast, stood on its prejudice in favor of a literal reading of the Bible's account of the monogenesis of the human race and rejected scientific racism.[19]

So I do believe that in the broad sense the War Between the States could be described as a religious war. But, like all religious wars, there were all sorts of other things mixed in with it. What could have been more of a religious war than the Crusades? And yet the historically informed can tell that a lot more than religion proper was involved in the Crusades. So it is with this—we were dealing with economic competition between the regions, different views of the Constitution, slavery, tariffs, divergent cultures, and differing religious faiths. All of that is readily acknowledged. It was a complex, messy situation.

The Influence of the Abolitionists

McKenzie says that we "greatly exaggerate the influence of abolitionists within the North as the war approached. (In this they mimic the paranoid views of many antebellum Southerners.)" He says a little later on the same page that we said the abolitionists were the "primary individuals beating 'the drums of war.'" This is yet another example of McKenzie over-egging the pudding. That is not what we said, although it is easier to debate with. We said

19. Eugene Genovese, *The Southern Tradition: The Achievement and Limitations of an American Conservatism* (Cambridge: Harvard Univ. Press, 1994), 27.

that the drums of war were being beaten by the abolitionists, and McKenzie inserted the word *primary* for us. This in itself is actually fine—it is what caricaturists do—but I object because I think he drew the nose in the wrong direction.

The position of the abolitionists in the North was comparable to the contemporary relationship between various leftist radicals and the Democratic Party. The radicals are not at the center, and yet they exert enormous influence on the Democrats. Lincoln was no abolitionist, and the Republican party was not the Abolitionist Party—just as we can say that the Democratic Party is *not* the Green Party or the Feminist Party. And yet, as with the relationship of Greens and radical feminists to the Democratic Party today, there was much willingness to use abolitionist propaganda when it suited the Republicans back then. Fogel and Engerman cite this example:

> Then in 1859 the Republican party converted Helper's book into a major ideological weapon of its presidential campaign. Condensed editions were published and a hundred thousand copies were distributed by the Republican party.[20]

This was a book that argued (erroneously) that the South was lagging far behind the North in material wealth and blamed the economic gap entirely on the institution of slavery. This sample bit of politics by the Republicans was not calculated to soothe the Southerner's "paranoia."

I grant that Lincoln was no abolitionist. If he could have fulfilled his agenda without freeing a single slave, he would have done so. On the question of race, he was a white supremacist, to use our current terminology. But his real agenda was the continuation of the goals of the defunct Whig party, an agenda of internal improvements, centralization, and so forth. He thought he could do this by means of a short war with the South that would remove some of the constitutional impediments that stood in his way.[21]

20. Fogel and Engerman, *Time on the Cross,* 161.
21. DiLorenzo, *The Real Lincoln,* 54–84.

But the war went on much longer than anticipated, and when he issued the Emancipation Proclamation (as a weapon of war), this became (in the minds of many) part of a revisionist justification for the war after the fact. But in fact the Emancipation Proclamation only freed slaves where the federal government had no control because it was Confederate-held territory, and it freed no slaves (not even those of General Grant) within Union territory. At the same time, Lincoln used the abolitionists in much the same way as Democrats use the Greens or contemporary Republicans use pro-lifers. Of course the political "using" was a two-way street, and the impact of all this on the Southerners was part of this equation.

McKenzie acknowledges that the Southerners were "paranoid" about abolitionist influence. But this is a form of influence, is it not? If the Southerners were sandbagging their way of life in order to prepare for the onslaught of the abolitionists, doesn't this mean that the abolitionists *had* influence? A central argument for the laws in the South that prohibited literacy for the slaves was the fear that abolitionist literature would get to them. This argument was roundly attacked by a Southern bishop in the Methodist Church (an attack I would echo and amen, by the way):

> If, he taunted, the Bible sanctions slavery, then slaveholders should want a Bible in every slave cabin in the South. Why, in any case, should Southerners make the blacks suffer for the sins of the Yankees? The periodicals of the several denominations echoed the sentiment.[22]

In sum, the kind of influence the abolitionists actually had is fully consistent with the claims we made concerning them in the booklet.

Proportion Again

In this disagreement he has had with us, extending over some years now, McKenzie has drawn the conclusion that I must have absolutely

---

22. Genovese, *A Consuming Fire*, 58.

no sense of proportion. For example, I said, "But because we have resolved to abandon sin, *this must include the sin of believing a lie.*"[23] McKenzie reasons thusly: "Since I am refusing to repent of believing what Wilson calls a lie, this must mean that he should logically consider me reprobate, and a fit subject of church discipline."

But allow a counter-example. Suppose I was preaching on the sin of sodomy, and I said something like this: "The Scriptures teach in Leviticus 19:22 that sodomy is an abomination, and all who contradict this are arguing with the God of heaven, and the wrath of God is visited upon them to the uttermost. Yea, verily, and amen." Now suppose one of the faithful in the congregation notices that I said Leviticus 19:22 when I should have said 18:22. Excitement of the moment, or slip of the tongue, fear of getting arrested, whatever. Now suppose further that this person was afraid to tell me I got the reference wrong, because in the second half of the sentence I had called down judgment from heaven on anyone who contradicted what I had said.

Such a person would either have to believe that I had virtually no sense of proportion, or *he* would have to have virtually no sense of proportion. The rhetoric in our booklet, which is quite vigorous and strong in places, is directed against those who are promoting sodomy, abortion, other monstrosities like that, as well as the Christians who let them. If McKenzie differed with me in the same ways that the kind of opponents *that I had in view* do (e.g., scoundrels here in Moscow in our current fracas, some of them professional historians)—that is, because he wanted the Church to start ordaining gays, then, yes, he should be disciplined. I say this because gnats and camels are different sizes.

McKenzie says that the *ad hominem* approach "teaches us that those who reach different intellectual conclusions from our own are simply truth-haters. Subliminally, at least, in reading books like *Southern Slavery as It Was*, we receive the message that there are simply no intellectually defensible grounds on which to differ with

23. Wilson and Wilkins, *Southern Slavery*, 8.

the authors." *Subliminally?* What is this? In the booklet we say that the mindset that says the "North represented nothing good" was infantile. We also say that there were godly Christians who fought for the North.[24] To say that a cause is generally suspect or even ignoble does not mean it can have no noble adherents or defenders. Why would we want to excommunicate a godly Christian *today* who approves of his great-grandfather who fought for the North (with *our* approval) back *then?* Why would I not excommunicate someone for joining the Union army and shooting at me, and then turn around and excommunicate McKenzie for simply differing with me? It makes no sense. McKenzie is honestly imagining things.

Again, the target of the strong rhetoric (as the context of the booklet makes plain) was the anti-God agenda of the current regime. When a homosexual couple move in next door to McKenzie, and they are just as married in the eyes of his state as McKenzie is, he should take note of the fact that we have been fighting this kind of thing for years. We could see it coming. Shoot, *Dabney* could see it coming. We *said* what we were aiming at, and it was zeal for the Word of God motivating us and not surplus testosterone. But McKenzie has persisted in maintaining that we must also (logically) be shooting at him too. Well, *we are not.* He should just come to grips with the fact that I would like to be friends with him.

Wild Inconsistencies

McKenzie spends a good bit of time showing the wild inconsistencies taken by various Southern states on issues relating to the role the federal government should have. I have no problem acknowledging this—just as New England states were all about secession themselves just a few decades earlier. A lot of the controversy, on both sides, was affected by whose ox was being gored.

What McKenzie has missed is that my primary identification is with my Christian brothers in the South, and not with "the South" generally. Genovese chronicles the frustrations that some of my

24. Ibid., 12.

theological heroes had as they tried to get their civil magistrates to bring the laws on slavery into some kind of decent conformity with the law of Scripture. As I read *A Consuming Fire*, I was filled with gratitude that so many of my Christian brothers were so faithful, over so many years, despite enormous obstacles, as they spoke the Word to the civil authority. But even so, the one blind spot that these Southern Christians all appeared to share, and which Genovese notes, is that they did not bring the sanctions of the church to bear. For example, if any church member separated a slave couple by selling one or both of them, in my view, that person should have been excommunicated. The Christians in the South had no need to wait around for the civil law. They should have been more eager to apply the Scriptures directly themselves, within their own ecclesiastical jurisdictions.

McKenzie said at the beginning of his paper that he teaches his students both "sympathy and skepticism" as they treat their historical subjects. But this is something at which Genovese excels, and which McKenzie has done poorly. Again, this lack of sympathy is for paradigm reasons, and not because I think McKenzie is a mean-spirited man. Reading Genovese's treatment of men like Thornwell and Dabney and McKenzie's treatment of men who so strongly identify with Thornwell and Dabney (e.g., me) is to experience two different interpretive worlds.

Black Confederates

McKenzie says that I make "the totally unsupportable claim that 40,000 slaves served as combatants in the Confederate Army." He answers this by quoting Clyde Wilson, a director in the League of the South. Wilson (that is, Clyde) says that a great many black Confederates helped sustain the armies and the home front, but "not as enrolled soldiers." But first, note the difference between "combatants" and "enrolled soldiers." It should also be noted that I said *blacks*, and not *slaves*. I know and said in my article that it is "true the Confederate *national* government did not approve the use of blacks under arms until late in the war, but the decentralized nature of the CSA must also be recognized."[25] I was not necessarily talking about enrolled soldiers, duly enlisted. I was talking about men who were in the fighting and who "saw the elephant"—men who actually did fight.

In *Credenda*, we had two pages of quotations which should be dealt with by more than a cavalier dismissal. The issue here is not whether my figure of 40,000 is dead on. I have heard estimates as high as 63,000, and of course it could be lower than 40,000, perhaps significantly so. But the issue is the way McKenzie argues *ex cathedra* here—with the simple use of the phrase *totally insupportable*. It is as though he said, "Back off, man, I'm a historian." But here is Frederick Douglass, the famous black abolitionist:

> There are at the present moment, many colored men in the Con-
> federate Army doing duty not only as cooks, servants, and laborers,
> but as real soldiers, having muskets on their shoulders and bullets
> in their pockets, ready to shoot down loyal troops and do all that
> soldiers may do to destroy the Federal government and build up
> that of the traitors and rebels.[26]

The Paradigm Thing

I wrote to McKenzie once that "there really is a Southern intellectual paradigm, and I am in it." He thought this was worse
than no explanation at all, and discussed Thomas Kuhn's book
on the structure of scientific revolutions. McKenzie then summarized Weaver's view that the Southern tradition had four pil-
lars, which were feudalism, chivalry, the idea of the gentleman,
and religious faith. Now there was *much more* to Weaver's book
than this, but let's take this as a very basic treatment. For more
extended discussion on this, and much else, consider my views

25. *Credenda/Agenda* 9.I: 5.
26. Quoted in Barrow, Segars, and Rosenburg, *Forgotten Confederates*, 10.

on medievalism,[27] chivalry and the idea of the gentleman,[28] and religious faith.[29]

I am a paleo-conservative. In my views on politics, government, social order, I have been affected in a thoroughly jumbled way by Augustine, Edmund Burke, Anselm, Russell Kirk, King Alfred, John Calvin, T. S. Eliot, John Knox, Thomas Jefferson, C. S. Lewis, J. R. R. Tolkien, G. K. Chesterton, and Robert E. Lee. I am not an ideologue—that is one of the things that principled conservatism stands against.

As an aside, the southern intellectual paradigm does not mean rejecting the practice of careful footnoting. For two examples, Weaver's book is filled with footnotes and M. E. Bradford conforms to current conventions also.[30] A third example occurs to me also—the Southern Agrarians were a remarkable collection of twentieth-century scholars, recognized as such, and they took a dim view of many of the same things that Steve Wilkins and I did. To use John Crowe Ransom's phrase, they were reconstructed but not regenerate, and that compromise with "reconstruction" allowed for footnotes.[31] This is the case with virtually all contemporary advocates of this paradigm I am defending.

Another straw man argument attacks a caricature of premodern thinking—"a 'premodern' description of slavery in which the facts don't matter." If this is read as saying that for premoderns the objective truth does not matter, it is simply false and a straw man misrepresentation. But if by this McKenzie means that in a premodern understanding there is a rejection of neutral "facts" sitting

27. Douglas Wilson and Douglas Jones, *Angels in the Architecture* (Moscow: Canon Press, 1998), and Douglas Wilson, *Recovering the Lost Tools of Learning* (Wheaton: Crossway Books, 1991).

28. Douglas Wilson, *Reforming Marriage* (Moscow: Canon Press, 1995) and *Future Men* (Moscow: Canon Press, 2001).

29. David Hagopian, ed., *Back to Basics* (Phillipsburg: Presbyterian and Reformed, 1996).

30. M. E. Bradford, *Remembering Who We Are* (Athens: Univ. of Georgia Press, 1985). This intellectual paradigm does, however, prevent religious awe of footnotes.

31. Twelve Southerners, *I'll Take My Stand*. See particularly the biographical notes on these men on pages 361–410.

out there, independent of the world the triune God actually made, he has pinpointed the heart of our disagreement. But I suspect he means the former.

This relates to the third objection that McKenzie anticipated from me. He believes that I would argue that despite the flaws, my argument is still true, and he dismisses this approach. An appropriate response to this is that *it depends*. To take a view that I will stick to my guns regardless of how many times and how many ways I have been shown to be wrong is simply being as stubborn as the Pope's mule. It is ungodly. But to maintain the center of your argument even if someone else shows that you were wrong on *incidental* things is not the same thing at all. This goes back to the earlier point about having a sense of proportion. When I acknowledge the possibility of errors in what I have written without conceding the central point, this is only reasonable. I fully expect McKenzie to do this also. For example, he has gotten a title wrong and a page number wrong in his discussion. But I know that the center of his argument does not depend on these things because I have a sense of proportion.

I also know that the center of his argument falls, because he does not really understand the arguments he is undertaking to criticize. But this latter problem is different than the former. No one should expect him to abandon his position because he got some incidental things wrong.

Epilogue

THIS BOOK HAS BEEN a collection of disparate elements organized around a set of common themes. Because the occasions for writing (or rewriting) them varied so much, their assembly into one book might have an ad-hoc, ragtaggy feel. But since it seems that I am now writing the epilogue, it is apparently too late.

The strength of presenting such a collection in book form is that it shows the *particular* nature of all such conflicts. In his great manifesto of Christian liberty called the book of Galatians, the apostle Paul took great pains to argue about the details of his travels, with special emphasis on how many times he had been to Jerusalem. In contrast, Euclid wrote a timeless book. There is no dust in it anywhere, which is frankly one of its shortcomings.

We have been embroiled in controversy for the last several years, and the issues addressed in this book have been a significant factor in that controversy. In the midst of all this, we have had some encouragement in the fact that we have been shot at from both extremes—from the radical left which thinks us guilty of manifest hate crimes, but also from the radical right, which is exasperated by our miscegenated compromises. In a strange fashion, this is a good indicator of Christian balance. Chesterton once commented that it "looked not so much as if Christianity was bad enough to include any vices, but rather as if any stick was good enough to beat Christianity with."[1]

Sometimes the sticks have been used on us by opposing factions, and sometimes *one* faction is worked up enough to use opposing sticks (happily unaware of the contradictions). But we are convinced that the reason for the uproar is that our *fundamental* allegiance is not any ideology, right or left, or to our nation, tribe, or political party. We are trinitarian Christians, and our absolute trust is in the Word of God. We are biblical absolutists. So the egalitarians are outraged because we say it was possible for a godly man to be a slave owner—because that is what the Bible says. And the white separatists are infuriated by us because we won't echo their follies on racial intermarriage—because the standard they advance is found nowhere in Scripture. We don't like the mosquitoes that come from any kind of fever swamp.

The grass withers, the flower fades, but the word of God endures forever (I Pet. I:24–25). Included in all those piles of withered grass are all nations, empires, parties, and revolutions—all the baubles that Satan tempted Jesus with in the wilderness. And the word of God, which endures forever, will summon His elect before the throne of the triune majesty—from every nation, tribe, race, and language, and there in that place we will all worship the Lamb.

I. G. K. Chesterton, *Orthodoxy* (New York: Doubleday, 1959), 88.

Appendix

In note 1 on page 59, I wrote that the footnoting errors in the original edition of Southern Slavery as It Was *were "atrocious." Since writing that, some accusations resulting from those errors have gained wider circulation and attention because of an article in* World *magazine. For that reason, we have included this appendix, the bulk of which is a post from my blog (at www.dougwils.com) explaining in more detail the nature of those atrocious footnotes.*

The WorldMagBlog food fight apparently continues, although everyone appears to be almost out of ammo. Steve Wilkins found out about the fracas after it had been going for several days and sent a statement (included below) to WorldMagBlog, which they posted under a separate thread. I am posting Steve's comments here in their entirety, and then want to follow them up with an amplification. The only part I differ with in Steve's comments is his attempt to exonerate me completely. Steve is one of the most honorable and conscientious Christian gentlemen I have ever met, and it is a great privilege to be his friend—although I have to say our mutual friendship has gotten us *both* in trouble. I am frankly surprised that our mothers still let us play together. Here is Steve's statement:

> I was surprised to learn of Mark Bergin's report about the "plagiarism" charge leveled against the booklet *Southern Slavery as It Was* (as noted on the *World Magazine* blog, April 23, 2005). This is not

exactly "breaking news" but if *World* wants to bring this up, it should desire to report the whole story and not simply repeat the charge itself.

The portion of the booklet that has been labeled "plagiarism" is totally my responsibility and not Doug Wilson's. That section of the booklet came straight from my lecture notes which were not referenced and I did not take the time to go through them carefully and reference them properly before submitting them to Doug for inclusion in the booklet. There was never any intent on my part to deceive or to present the material from Drs. Fogel and Engerman as my own. I always made plain in my lectures that this material was drawn from the study of Drs. Fogel and Engerman and as I have never studied the plantation records on which their study was based (indeed, I have never even seen any plantation records of any sort!), I am completely unqualified to make any of the judgments or to draw any of the conclusions presented in the booklet. All of it came straight out of *Time on the Cross.*

Though it may be acceptable simply to note this verbally in a lecture so that all understand the source of the material, it is utterly inappropriate and inexcusable not to make plain your sources when you publish your material. I should have been more careful and taken the time to properly reference the material in my section of the pamphlet. I did not do this and thus, fully deserve all the blame for this sloppy, inexcusable, and unjustifiable action.

Doug Wilson's only fault was that he trusted his friend to be responsible and careful. Thus, one might sympathize with my astonishment that he would be blamed for something he didn't do. Well, I should say I'm not really astonished that those who hate the gospel and are filled with blind prejudice would do this—indeed, this is perfectly consistent with the actions of those lovers of "tolerance" in the Moscow community over the last three years or so. But what can we expect? They love lies and are acting just like their father. As my grandmother used to say, "they can't help it if they act ugly." What is truly incredible to me, however, is that those who present themselves as faithful Christians, responsible journalists, and knowledgeable seminary professors, would so quickly and thoughtlessly take the side of the enemy with so little consideration and regard for the whole story (not to mention their indifference to the broader context of this entire fracas). It is enough to give one "pause" as they say.

Thus, I find myself in the embarrassing position of having my friend take all the blame for my sin. I will not stand for it any longer. Therefore I protest, and hereby insist on taking my fair share of the blame—and as far as this particular story is concerned, that means that I should get it all.

The part I disagree with is his Steve's use of that last word "all." Steve and I both wrote our respective sections and are each responsible for their respective contents. But at the same time, I was the one who edited them, putting them together in one sustained piece. The booklet was not a "two article" affair, with his name on his and mine on mine. There was one sustained argument from front to back. Both our names were on the cover. And I was the one who had the editorial responsibility for blending them. And even if this *had* been a "two article" booklet, I still would have been the editor, and an essential part of a good editor's responsibility is to anticipate the possibility of this kind of error, and check on it. Accidents do happen, and an editor's responsibility includes an active *awareness* of the fact that accidents happen, and to therefore *check*. I didn't check, and I should have. *Mea maxima culpa.* I had not read *Time on the Cross* at that time, and given the nature of the errors, had I read that book we would have been spared a lot of grief. Further, given the controversial nature of the point we were making, it was absolutely essential that *no* handles be presented to our adversaries. But those handles were presented anyway, and it was not just Steve's responsibility that this happened. The responsibility was also mine.

So I am not printing Steve's comments above as a way of sidling away from him. I have wanted to own my responsibilities in this throughout—and I did so publicly on this blog last summer. First, my association with Steve was as co-author and editor, and we were and are on the same team. And nothing is more unseemly than members of the same team trying to blame one another when things go wrong. When the right-fielder starts blaming the left-fielder, they have quit playing the other team and have started to play each other, which means that defeating them will be easy. And second, Steve is a good personal friend and one thing I sure as hell wasn't going to do is back away from him just because I could tell a plausible story about it, a story that would sell in these individualistic times. It would sell out there, but it would be a stench before God. And in an aside to the pietists, if I might paraphrase C. S. Lewis, my use of "sure as hell" was not frivolous swearing. Given that the lake of fire is reserved for liars, among others, the sureness of hell is something that more than a few active participants in our slander wars out here ought to be contemplating.

more from Canon Press

Read this title in full online at www.canonpress.com.

The first biblical argument against racism is found in the Deca-
logue. The sixth commandment forbids us to take the life of
another. Christ argues that the implications of this commandment are far deeper than overt murder. The Lord teaches us that
the commandment also condemns vile mockery and unexpressed
hateful heart attitudes (Mt. 5:21–22). He rescues this law from
those who had clouded it with their human traditions.

The Westminster Larger Catechism expounds the sixth
commandment as forbidding, among other things, "sinful anger,
hatred, envy, desire of revenge . . . provoking words, oppression
. . . striking, wounding, and whatsoever else tends to the destruction of the life of any" (Q. 136). If we are forbidden to have or act
on hateful attitudes toward anyone, then we are forbidden from
doing such things to an individual of another race.

Moreover, the Larger Catechism explains that the sixth commandment obligates us to preserve the life of others "by chari-
table thoughts, love, compassion, meekness, gentleness, kindness;
peaceable, mild and courteous speeches and behavior; forbear-
ance, readiness to be reconciled, patient bearing and forgiving of
injuries, and requiting good for evil; comforting and succouring the
distressed, and protecting and defending the innocent" (Q. 135).
Racist attitudes stand in stark contrast to these prescriptions. The
law of God goes to the heart of the issue. To be a racist is to be a
killer.

the biblical offense of racism
by Douglas Jones

CPSIA information can be obtained
at www.ICGtesting.com
Printed in the USA
LVHW030150300822
727118LV00013B/920

9 781591 280323